SUCCESSFUL MATH
STUDY SKILLS

SUCCESSFUL MATH STUDY SKILLS

**Easy-to-use / Step-by-Step Guide
to Higher Math Grades**

For Middle and Secondary
School Students

Paul Nolting Ph.D.
William A. Savage M.S.

ACADEMIC SUCCESS PRESS, INC.
POMPANO BEACH, FLORIDA

SUCCESSFUL MATH STUDY SKILLS

BY PAUL D. NOLTING & WILLIAM A. SAVAGE

Published by Academic Success Press, Inc.

Cover Design by Wright & Ratzlaff Associates

Printed in the United States of America

Second Edition

First Printing

ISBN: 0-940287-18-8

ACKNOWLEDGMENTS

This book could not have been written without the help and support of many people. The authors gratefully acknowledge the following partial list of those we are indebted to: Pat Ahearn, Shirley Aver, Pauline Bostick, John Casey, Barb Cyphers, George Douglas, Downey Dutterer, Beverly Folds, Lynda Foster, Catherine Frank, Carol Freidman, Brenda Hiers, Shirley Holm, Kaye Holmes, Pam Inman, Linda Jones, Bobbie Kantner, Gale Klein, Judy Krieling, Ora Lang, Betty Larson, Gil Loeser, Barb Maechtle, Tawnya Matis, Keith Mathias, Gary Mitchell, Sue Pantling, Dr. E. Ray Phillips, Rose Phillips, Carolann Richardson, Louis Robinson, Barbara Shoop, Carol Sicard, Joann Sizemore, Robert Stewart, Virginia Taylor, Afra Wade and Mike Wilder .

We are especially grateful to Dr. Mary McClendon, Supervisor of Mathematics, Sarasota County Public Schools and Arthur Dotterweich, Supervisor of Mathematics, Manatee County Public Schools for their encouragement and support.

A special word of thanks to Sandra Jessee, of S^3, for her efficient typing, proof reading and dedication to the book.

We thank Jim Hanson, of Second Avenue Publishing, for his computer knowledge and innovative style in getting the book ready for printing.

Lastly we thank our wives, Vickie Nolting and Joanne Savage, for their proof reading and editing skills, patience and total support.

Table of Contents

PREFACE

This book is written for middle and secondary school students for the purpose of improving math study skills. It is intended to be used by math students prior to or while taking algebra. But the concepts contained in this book can be used effectively at any grade level, 5 through 12.

Learning to be a good math student is like learning to be a good parent. No one tells you how but everyone expects you to be perfect. Wouldn't it be nice if classes were offered to help teach adults how to be good parents? Think of all the problems parents have to face with absolutely no training. And then think about the similarity of studying math correctly, with no training.

Before we go on, let me ask you, the reader, some important questions.

"When was the last time some one taught you how to take a test?" For most students, the answer is probably never. Yet, you know how important it is to learn to take a test correctly. Test grades, after all, are averaged to give the student a final grade. So, here's an important skill to learn, no question about it!

A few more questions:

"When was the last time someone taught a student how to take good notes?" "Do you copy everything down word for word from the board?" "Do you write down important ideas?" "Or what do you do?"

Last question:

"Has anyone ever explained to a student the difference between studying math and studying other subjects like social studies or English?" Most math teachers will say, "Math is a foreign language." For instance, what would happen if you decided to study French this year and started the first day in a French 4 class rather than a French 1 class? You wouldn't be able to read the textbook. Taking math is similar to studying a foreign language. There are new symbols to recognize, learn to pronounce, understand, and use when solving problems.

Skills like test taking, listening, note taking, time management and memory are important to understanding mathematics. These skills will be a part of the final grade received for studying mathematics. The important idea to remember is that math study skills can be learned. These skills are not mysterious. They are skills learned easily, step-by-step.

If a student has been a poor math student in the past, chances are that he/she has never learned how to study math correctly. If a student has been a good math student in the past, learning the proper math study skills will enable him/her to keep good grades in math or improve math grades. In short, this math study skills text is for students at all math abilities and grades.

To The Teacher

As a teacher of mathematics, one of your main goals has always been to have your students gain complete and total understanding of the math course. There are three main ingredients that enable you to accomplish this task.

First, and most important, your students must have the prerequisite entry level skills necessary to pass your course. But fortunately or unfortunately, you will have little or no control over entry level skills. If a student shows up in your class on opening day in middle school or high school, you would have to assume that the student has satisfied the minimum requirements of the preceding course.

Secondly, be aware of the fact that the quality of your instruction also plays a part in the student's understanding of the material presented. Attending professional meetings, workshops and conference, and taking graduate level math classes will help you improve your quality of instruction.

Lastly, teaching your students math study skills will play a very important role in their successful understanding of the material and course completion. Most students do not know how to study math. That is understandable. No one ever taught them how to study math. It is true, of course, that many good instructors teach math study skills. However, most math instructors were never formally taught math study skills. It is also true that instructors teach study skills when time permits, not really focusing on all the skills available and necessary, and rarely in an organized and timely manner. This book, either as a separate course or as part of your regular curriculum, will improve your student's understanding and grades.

Some high schools use this book as the text for a separate course in math or general study skills, while others have taught the material one or two days per week. Teachers have taught this material each day for the first five to nine weeks, depending on the length of the period.

Middle school teachers have included the course in their wheel, either as an elective or a required course of study. Other seventh and eighth grade teachers have used a team approach.

There are as many ways as there are imaginative teachers to present this material. The choice is yours. The most important concept to remember is that math study skills are important to your students. Find a way that works best for you and your school to present this material to your students. Academic Success Press, Inc. guarantees that the improvement in student understanding and grades will make you as happy as it has so many others.

CHAPTER 1
What is Math and Why is It Different

1

What is math and why is it different?

A brief discussion on what math is seems appropriate for a math study skills text. It has often been said that we learn best if we know why we have to learn it.

Math means different things to different people but most mathematicians will agree...

Math is a way of thinking.

Math is a study of related ideas.

Math is a language.

Math is a tool.

Math is a philosophy.

Math is an art.

Math is a Way of Thinking

Math as a way of thinking is covered in more detail in Chapter II. It is important to realize that learning to think and learning to organize thoughts are a major part of math.

Math is a Study of Related Ideas

Math as a study of related ideas is obvious when we look at the transition between the various branches of mathematics. For example, arithmetic, algebra, geometry and trigonometry are not taught as independent courses. Common ideas run through all courses. Skills learned in previous courses are needed to master concepts and ideas in the next higher level math course.

Math is a Language

Math is a foreign language. Look at the next higher level math book. Arithmetic students, for example, would not be able to understand an elementary algebra book. An algebra I student would have difficulty understanding an algebra II book. A trigonometry student would have difficulty reading a calculus book. Math has its own shorthand. It is made up of symbols and abbreviated words. Math has its own vocabulary and sentence structure. Math can be considered a foreign language.

Math is a Tool

Many students see math as a tool. They believe that the real purpose of understanding math is to help students in other subjects such as chemistry, biology and physics. Math as a tool is just another name for math.

Math is a Philosophy

Math as a philosophy becomes clear when looking at the history of mathematics. Math has its own set of definitions, rules, axioms and theorems used to draw logical conclusions. Many mathematicians would support the idea that the same arguments used in deductive proofs in geometry are used in philosophy and law. Math as a philosophy has been developing for hundreds of years.

Math is an Art

Lastly, math is an art. This is especially true when you look at beautiful geometric designs. These designs are in both plane and solid geometry, and can be seen in the world around us. For example, columns supporting buildings, floor tile patterns, some bridges and the great pyramids of Egypt, all use designs from the field of mathematics. Some students even see a detailed algebraic proof, with step-by- step calculations, as art.

Three characteristics or traits of mathematics make it different from studying other courses.

1. Most students fail to realize that studying math is much like studying a foreign language. Math has its own set of rules, theorems, laws and grammar.

2. Learning math depends on previously learned math skills. For example, what we learned yesterday will be used in today's lesson, and what we learn today will be used in tomorrow's lesson, and so on.

3. Math is a skill subject. You can not learn math by listening or watching. You must learn math by practicing it. Just like any sport, you must practice it to improve your skill.

Let's take a closer look at all three special characteristics of math.

Math is a Language

One of the biggest differences between mathematics and courses like social studies is that math is a language. Students need to realize this special characteristic of math. Students must learn to study math like they study a foreign language. Think about all the symbols used in mathematics from the equal sign (=), used in arithmetic, to the summation sign (Σ) used in calculus. Symbols are used such as inclusion ([ ]), greater than (>), square root ($\sqrt{}$), absolute value (| |), union ($\cup$), empty set (ϕ), and factorial (!). The list goes on and on.

Not only do students have to remember symbols and how to pronounce them, but students also have to learn abbreviations for math words. Take for example a unit on logarithms studied in an algebra II class in high school. How would you pronounce Log10? What does it mean? Imagine the difficulty trying to answer a math question when you can not read it correctly.

Several good methods are used to learn how to pronounce math terms. When the teacher introduces a new symbol or word, pronounce the symbol or word to yourself over and over until you say it exactly like your teacher. Foreign language teachers use the same technique with their language students.

Second, save some pages in the back of your notebook to record new words or symbols.

Write down each new word or symbol (be sure you can pronounce it) with the formal definition given by your teacher or your math book. Now write the definition in your own words. If you can not write the definition in your own words, you don't understand it.

Before your next test write new symbols or words on 3 x 5 inch cards with definitions and applications on the back of the card. Review these cards by yourself or with another student. Keep practicing until you can define, give one application, and pronunciate each new word, concept, or symbol.

Another important idea about math as a foreign language is this: We do not hear or read about the language of mathematics in our daily lives. We obtain information about the world from newspapers, radio and television. However, math formulas, math symbols or math concepts are not part of news stories. The only places you learn how to speak the special language of math is in a math classroom and when practicing your homework. You need to keep this special characteristic about math in mind.

"YOU DO NOT HEAR DAN RATHER ON TV
TALKING IN MATHEMATICS FORMULAS"

Reading involves learning how to pronounce the words, understanding the words, and being able to apply what you have read to appropriate situations.

1. Since math is a language, you first must know how to pronounce the new words and symbols.

2. You must know the meaning of the new words and symbols.

3. You must know how to apply the new words and symbols.

When you realize that math is a foreign language it helps you to study and learn the math with greater ease.

Math is Sequential

When you first meet with a math class a teacher should tell their students, "Don't miss a class, not a single class, for the rest of the school year."

Why?

Research has shown a high relationship between math grades and attendance. This means that students who are frequently absent from math class will usually have very poor grades and can fail the course. The same thing can happen if you attend class but do not pay attention to the instruction.

In other subjects such as history or English, absences will cause lower grades but not to the same extent as math. The reason absences affect math students so much is that math is sequential. This means learning new material is based on knowing previously studied material.

FOR EXAMPLE: an algebra student, who continues to have problems with fractions, will have more serious problems when trying to solve fractional equations taught in the next chapter.

Learning math has sometimes been compared to constructing a building from the ground up. The blocks used to make the foundation have to be complete and strong. What would happen if, on every layer of blocks, a few were missing? It would not take long for the house to fall down!

The same is true about math. We must continue to learn math each day because new material is constantly being presented. Without a good understanding of the previous day's work, new material becomes more difficult to comprehend. When new material is not completely learned a weak foundation is formed for learning future math material. The results of not learning your new math and skills is to fail math.

Being successful in a math course is like being successful in anything else you do. It takes time and effort. You need to decide from the very first day to...

1. Attend class.
2. Pay attention.
3. Make every effort to practice math every school day.

Math is a Skill Subject

From as far back as one can remember, teachers have told students that math is a skill subject. Math is similar in many ways to learning to play a musical instrument or learning to type. You can listen or watch your instructor for as long as you please. But unless you practice typing or playing the instrument yourself, you will not learn.

Think about it. Suppose you wanted to learn to play the piano and hired the best available teacher. You sit next to your teacher on the bench. Since your teacher is a good teacher, you will understand exactly what is told to you about the notes on the page and the keys on the piano. But what does it take to learn to play the piano? You, yourself, have to place your fingers on the keyboard and begin to practice.

Math works the same way. You can go to class, listen to your math teacher and understand everything that is said. That is, all the examples written on the board seem clear and there is no doubt in your mind about any of the material. But if you then leave class and do not practice by working math problems, you will never learn math.

Many subjects or parts of subjects can be learned by methods other than doing. For example, in social studies, information can be learned by listening to your instructor, taking good notes and perhaps by engaging in a lively group discussion. Math is different. If you want to learn math, *YOU MUST PRACTICE*. And practice means not only doing your homework but also understanding the reasons for each problem step.

In other words, you must remember the three special characteristics of math that make studying math different from other subjects:

1. Remember that math is a language.
2. Remember that math is sequential.

3. Remember that math is a skill that will help you become successful in math.

Now that we have discussed <u>why</u> math is different from other subjects, let's look at <u>how</u> to make math <u>work for you</u>.

Summer School vs. School Year

Many schools offer students the opportunity of attending summer school. However, math courses taught during the summer are more difficult to learn than those taught during the regular school year. The problem is the amount of material presented each day and the necessary amount of homework time needed for understanding the material.

Since summer school is taught over a short period of time, students are required to attend class two or more hours per day. Though students receive the same amount of classroom time, two or three times the amount of material is covered each day. This, of course, means two or three times the amount of homework to do for each day. Also, with longer classes, students who get "lost" during the first half hour are "lost" for the remainder of the class. To decrease the chance of getting lost, some students need to read ahead in the textbook. This further increases homework time.

It is easy to understand why some summer school students fall behind quickly. The problem with summer school is that students who fall behind do not have enough time to recover. For this reason, summer school is not recommended.

Course Understanding and Grades

Since math is sequential, it is important to have a good understanding of each math course before taking the next higher level math course. This means earning a final grade of an "A", "B" or high "C". A passing grade of "D" is not a predictor of success. A "D" means a student does not have a good understanding of the math course taken and, therefore, the next higher level math course will be more difficult. (Remember, you can still be successful at the next higher level math course by improving your entry level skills through a good review during the summer months.)

Your First Math Test

Making a high grade on the first major math test is more important than making a high grade on the first major test in other subjects. The first major math test is the easiest. Meanwhile, far too many students feel that the first major math test is mainly review and they can make a "B" or "C" without much study. These students are overlooking a fine opportunity to make an "A" on the easiest major math test of the year. The first test counts the same as the more difficult remaining major math tests.

Students who fail to study for this first test often do not pass the math course or do not make the math grade they want. The reason is because their first major test grade was not high enough to pull up a low test score on one of the remaining major tests.

Studying hard for your first major math test and obtaining an "A" has several advantages.

- A high score on this first math test can make up for a low score on a more difficult fourth or fifth math test - and major tests count the same.

- A high score on this first test tells you that you have learned the basic math skills required to pass the course. This means you will not have to spend more time relearning the misunderstood material covered on the first major test. You can just learn the new material for the next test.

- A high score on this first test tends to improve motivation. Improved motivation can cause you to increase your math study time which allows you to master new material.

- A high score on this first test improves confidence. With more confidence you are more likely to work harder on the difficult math homework problems.

This effort will increase your chances of doing well in the course.

Finding a Study Buddy

One of the easiest ways to improve your understanding of mathematics and earn higher grades is by finding a study buddy. A study buddy is someone you can study with or call on the phone if you need help on a math problem.

It is helpful to study with someone. If you can not answer a question, maybe your study buddy can. If you both are having trouble with a question, perhaps each of you will remember enough from the class lesson to solve the problem together.

One way to solve a problem together is for each of you to take a turn talking out loud about the problem. Talking out loud can trigger the other person's memory on how to do the problem. This can also help you find out where you got stuck on the problem.

Remember, you need to use your study time wisely and concentrate on your math. Be aware of two dangers when studying together.

1. Not much math gets done when you start talking about next week's dance or last Saturday's football game, etc.

2. If your math assignment has twenty questions, for example, do not fall into the trap of doing questions 1 - 10 and your study buddy doing questions 11- 20. You both must work on question number 1 and then question number 2, etc., until you get the right answers supported by correct work.

Another way to work together is to have both of you try to complete the homework before you meet. Then, you can go over your answers and help each other on the problems you could not complete. It has often been said that two heads are better than one. This is especially true when doing your math homework with a study buddy.

SUMMARY

Math means different ideas to different people. But most people agree that math is a way of thinking, a study of related ideas, a language, a tool, a philosophy and an art.

The three characteristics that make math different:

1. Math is a language.
2. Math is sequential.
3. Math is a skill subject.

Summer school is not a good choice for taking a math course. The amount of material presented each day and the necessary amount of homework time needed for understanding the material makes it more difficult.

Because math is sequential, it is important to have a good understanding of each math course before continuing on to the next higher level math course. A "D" in your last math course means you will have great difficulty in your current math course.

Your first math test is important in determining your final grade. Be sure to study hard for it.

Finding a study buddy can be very helpful in under standing your math course and earning a higher grade. Working together on your math problems can improve your success.

HOMEWORK EXERCISES

1. Math means different ideas to different people. State at least six ideas as to what math is. Can you come up with any others? If so, list them.

2. List the three characteristics of math that make math different from other subjects.

3. State in your own words why math is considered to be a language.

4. What does the statement, "Math is sequential," mean?

5. Why have the authors stated that math is a skill subject? Give an example.

6. List two main reasons why taking math in summer school is more difficult than taking math during the regular school year?

7. State in your own words why it is important to have a good understanding of each math course taken.

8. List four reasons for doing well on your first math test.

9. Do you agree that studying with a study buddy is helpful? Explain your answer.

CHAPTER 2

Reasons to Study Math

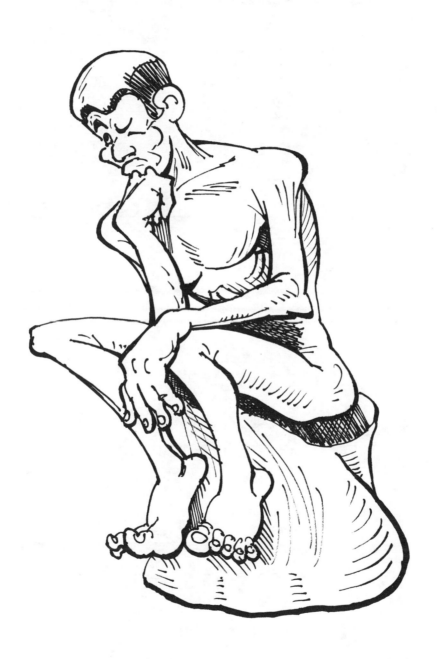

2

"Why do I have to study math?" is a question all too often asked. The question not only comes from students who find math difficult but from bright students as well. Students will do better at math, if they know the many good reasons for being successful in math.

The Arithmetic Program

To answer the question, "Why take math?" let's look at the math program through grade 8. In most schools the main emphasis through grade 8 (excluding accelerated algebra classes) is to finish the arithmetic program. Whole numbers, fractions, decimals and percents are taught but with a higher degree of difficulty than in earlier grades. Some schools will also teach pre-algebra and geometry units.

Lessons learned through 8th grade math are used over and over again in the *real world*. Shop at any department store and you will see sale signs which say 1/4th off. Determine how much sales tax at 7 percent you will pay on an item. Measure a room to determine how much paint to buy. These are examples of how you use what you have learned in math through grade 8. We all use arithmetic and some simple geometric relationships many times over in our daily lives. Therefore, one of the reasons for taking math through grade 8 is the need to learn *real world* math skills.

Math Beyond Arithmetic

What about high school math then? What about taking all those college calculus classes? What are the reasons for taking math beyond arithmetic?

Solving quadratic equations in a high school algebra class and covering a lengthy and complex lesson, something like $2X^2 + X = 6$, seems far from the real world. You don't see quadratic equations when shopping at the local super market. Why do we need to learn to solve quadratic equations? Why do we need to learn about more difficult math such as trigonometry, etc.?

The answer to these questions can be divided into four additional areas.

Some students are interested in careers in engineering, architecture, and the sciences. For this group, the answer is easy; they will use math in performing job tasks.

For students not pursuing a career that is math oriented, the answer is also easy. *Learning math teaches us how to think and how to organize our thoughts.*

Math is one of the few courses where we are constantly learning new procedures. These new procedures enable students to solve more and more difficult problems. Before too many years, math students have many rules, formulas and step-by-step operations stored away in their minds. This information is ready to be used to answer a particular problem.

Good math students are forever looking at a problem, deciding what rules apply, then deciding which rule to use first.

Let's take a look at a very simple arithmetic example:

Judy had ten apples, gave three to her brother and one to her friend. How many apples did she have left?

To solve this problem you have to select the operations from your math knowledge which apply here. Then, you must decide which operation to use first, which to use second, and so on.

We constantly use this kind of organized thinking in our day-to-day lives when solving real world problems. Let's illustrate this point with a story.

Suppose you are driving a car and suddenly get a flat tire. You pull over, stop, open your trunk and see lots of tools there, including a shovel, screw driver, tire iron, jack, etc. After seeing what tools are available, you select the proper tools to use. Next, you decide which tool to use first, which to use second and so on.

Does this thinking process sound familiar? Of course, it does. Math teaches us how to learn to think and organize our thoughts.

Some algebra students will never use the methods learned for solving quadratic equations. But all math students will benefit by practicing their thinking and organizational skills, all of which can be used in non-math situations.

Graduation Requirements

If the above reasons do not convince you that math is important, here is a more practical or realistic reason. In middle school and high school, you must have a certain number of math credits to graduate.

In Florida high schools, a student must have three math credits to graduate and must pass a state math test. In other high schools, students must pass algebra I to graduate. Many students have difficulty passing their high school math course because they did not learn enough arithmetic in middle school.

Good and poor math students sometimes spend too much time arguing why math is important or not important. If these students would put the same amount of time into learning how to learn math, they would be far better off.

Remember: To graduate from school you must pass math. So, let's work together in learning how to learn math in order to help you reach your highest math level and graduate.

Getting a Good Job

Graduating from high school may be a few months or years away. Some students have difficulty looking beyond graduation. Other students see high school as a step to a good job, further education or the armed services. But too few students realize that barely passing their high school math courses means getting lower paying jobs.

Since jobs are becoming more technical (requiring more math knowledge), employers do not want to employ poor math students.

The armed forces will take any high school graduate. But the students with good math skills have a better chance of selecting the better training areas in the armed forces. These better training areas can lead to better jobs when you leave the armed forces.

Students who do not have algebra II will have little or no chance to attend a university. These students can attend a community college or junior college, but these students will most likely start with non-credit courses. Students who did not have algebra I in high school will usually take 3 to 5 college non-credit and credit math courses.

Being successful in upper level math courses will start you on your way to a successful life.

Poor math skills, like it or not, lead to low paying jobs and limited training. Success in math, on the other hand, will open many job and educational opportunities.

SUMMARY

Students take math courses to learn how to think in an organized manner.

Students take math through the arithmetic program, with some elementary geometry, because this math is used in our daily lives.

All students must pass math courses in middle school and high school to graduate.

Students who have good math skills will be able to obtain better jobs and have a choice of post-high school training areas. Students with poor math skills will have fewer chances of getting good jobs and a university education.

Some students take math through high school and college because this math is needed as part of a career choice such as engineering, architecture, teaching, etc. Other students take math courses throughout high school and college because they enjoy the subject. No matter if you like math or not, it is the key to many high paying jobs and excellent educational opportunities.

HOMEWORK EXERCISES

1. Write a paragraph about the kind of career you would like to have when you graduate from high school or college. Will mathematics play a part in your plans?

2. List 5 reasons why you should study math. Can you think of any others?

3. Why is mathematics important to you through the arithmetic and elementary geometry programs?

4. If you do not think you will use the skills learned in math courses in your adult life, why are you required to take math beyond grade 8?

5. Explain this statement: Students with poor math skills will usually have lower paying jobs after high school.

6. Explain this statement: Students with poor math skills might not be able to go to the college of their choice.

Notes:

CHAPTER 3
Identifying Your Learning Strengths and Weaknesses

3

Being successful at math depends on several factors:
1. Previous math knowledge.
2. Level of test anxiety.
3. Study habits.
4. Study attitudes.
5. Motivation and test taking skills.

But before we start identifying your strengths and weaknesses, you need to understand what leads to success in *all* courses.

Dr. Benjamin Bloom, a well known researcher in the field of education, found that three major areas contribute to a student's final grade. (See Figure I). Fifty percent of the grade comes from I.Q. (intelligence) and entry level skills. Entry level skills are the skills you already have in that subject. Twenty-five percent of your grade is accounted for by quality of instruction. The final twenty-five percent of your grade is determined by a student's personal characteristics.

I.Q. (ability to learn) is made up of a person's capacity to reason and to understand difficult ideas. Over your life-time your I.Q. will not change much.

Entry level skills could be described as a store of knowledge gained from previous math courses. One teacher defines entry level skills as how much a student knew about a subject when first starting the course.

Quality of instruction focuses on how well a teacher can present lessons in the classroom. Quality of instruction also includes items such as course textbook, tutoring, and audio-visual equipment used.

A student's personal characteristics are characteristics that affect their ability to learn. Personal characteristics include attitudes about school, anxiety, study habits, motivation and test taking skills.

Figure 1
Variables contributing to student academic achievement

Entry Level Skills

Intelligence and entry level skills play a major role in your understanding of math and your final grade. Be certain that when you start a new math course your entry level skills are at or above the level needed to be successful. If you are unsure about your entry level math skills, talk to your teacher.

There are several ways to improve your math entry level skills. *Review your last math course material before starting your present math course.*

Teachers always think you finished your last math course last week. Teachers will not wait for you to catch up on current material. This attitude is understandable in both middle school and high school. Teachers are required to teach a certain amount of material during the year and can not wait for you to catch up.

Many good teachers will review at the beginning of a course but soon must start teaching new material. You should review your previous math course material before starting your new math course.

One of the best ways to review is to ask your teacher if you can borrow the math book you used during the year for study in the summer months. If you can not borrow a text, then go to a bookstore and buy a new or used math book. Have your teacher mark the chapters you need to review. Set up a time schedule so that you review each chapter as you prepare for your Fall math course. Remember to review during the entire summer. However, you should especially review the last few weeks before the Fall semester begins.

Another way in which to improve your entry level skills is to save tests and homework from your last math course. When most students get their tests back from their instructor, they discard them. Think how valuable it would be to you to have all your tests in one place. These tests would be the start of an excellent summer review as you prepare for next year's course.

Save your homework too. If you do your homework in a note book, the task of saving your homework is made easier. Many teachers will say that the course is the homework exercises. Since this tends to be true, saving and reviewing your homework will help you improve your entry level skills.

One last way to improve your entry level skills is to get some additional help from a tutor. This is especially important if you just barely passed your last math course.

Tutoring does not always have to be expensive. Sometimes a good friend, who is also a good math student, will help. Sometimes an older brother or sister, who already passed the course, will give some tutoring help. If you need professional tutoring, the best tutor would be your math teacher. Your school counselor may also suggest some other professional tutors.

One thing to keep in mind during the school year is that most teachers always find a few minutes after school to help a sincere and well motivated student. Take advantage of help when it is offered to insure adequate entry level skills.

Quality of Instruction

The quality of instruction plays an important part in determining your understanding of math and your grade in any math course. Classroom atmosphere, instructor's teaching style, textbook layout and information, all of these can all affect your ability to learn in the classroom.

The ideal situation is for teaching styles to match your learning style.

Your learning style is based on how you learn best. Some students like to hear things or see things.

To help you learn best, ask your counselor about measuring your learning style. Fortunately or unfortunately, students have little or no choice of math teachers in the middle or high school grades. Therefore, you need to expand your learning styles to learn the maximum amount of material from each of your teachers.

Do not be afraid to talk to your teachers about course rules, grading, policies and timing of material presented. Teachers welcome input from their students. Always remember, however, your math learning problems are easier to discuss on a respectful one-to-one basis.

Personal Characteristics

Of the major areas discussed that affect your math grade, which areas do you have some control over?

Your intelligence will remain pretty much the same throughout your life. Assuming you passed your previous math course, you should have the minimum entry level skills to be successful in your present math course. (Remember: I.Q. and entry level skills determine fifty percent of your math grade.)

The quality of instruction is generally beyond your control. Therefore, it is your instructor's responsibility to present effective lessons (twenty-five percent of your math grade).

The one area remaining, which accounts for the last twenty-five percent of your math grade, involves your personal characteristics.

This area includes math study habits, test taking skills, time management, reading and note taking procedures, and homework. You can improve your understanding of math and raise your math grade by making changes in your personal characteristics.

In the chapters ahead you will find detailed information on how to improve your personal math learning characteristics.

Most math students are not taught how to improve their personal math characteristics until they reach college. Take this opportunity to learn how to improve your math studies by changing your personal math characteristics.

Identifying Your Strengths and Weaknesses

Students have good and poor mathematics learning characteristics which affect their course grade. For example, developing good study skills is a mathematics learning characteristic, while high test anxiety is a poor mathematics learning characteristic.

To understand your learning strengths and weaknesses, your school may be able to provide you with one or more of the following standardized tests:

* Mathematics Anxiety Rating Scale (MARS)
* Survey of Study Habits and Attitudes (SSHA)
* Nowicki-Strickland Locus of Control (NSLC)
* The reading part of the Stanford Achievement Test
* The mathematics portion of the Wide Range Achievement Test (WRAT).

These tests are used throughout the United States. If you take these tests, they will give you a clear idea of your strengths and weaknesses. Ask your teacher or counselor if these tests are available.

A Student Profile Sheet (Figure 2) is included at the end of this chapter for you to copy. Record your scores on it should you be able to complete any of the surveys or tests.

Also found at the end of this chapter are a number of student profiles (Figures 3, 4, 5, 6, and 7). These profiles show how identifying strengths and weaknesses relates to improving grades in mathematics.

From these profiles, it can be seen that students have different reasons for being unsuccessful in math. If you can not take the suggested tests and surveys, a Math Study Skills Evaluation is provided.

A test anxiety symptoms list is also provided to help you understand your learning strengths and weaknesses.

The Math Study Skills Evaluation is found at the end of this chapter. Be sure not to write in this book. When you are ready to take the Math Study Skills Evaluation, use your own paper. When you finish the evaluation, ask your teacher to help you with the score.

Test Anxiety Symptoms

Many students suffer from test anxiety. Have you ever started a test and immediately felt ill? If so, you could have test anxiety.

Some of the symptoms are being nervous, having sweaty palms, having a faster than normal heart beat, having an uneasy feeling in your stomach and sometimes getting physically sick. Other symptoms include not remembering facts that you knew or taking a long time to remember those facts. Walking out of a test and then remembering how to do the problem is another symptom. If you suffer from even one or two of these symptoms, you have a degree of test anxiety. Having too much test anxiety means you will not do your best on a test and, therefore, will not get the grade that you deserve.

Test anxiety is important. Give test anxiety your special attention. This important material on reducing test anxiety is found in Chapter 5.

MATH STUDY SKILLS EVALUATION - H

(Students Note: Use your own paper for this evaluation. Number your paper from 1 to 20.)
Read each of the items below. Choose the statement in each group which is true of you. Indicate what you actually do rather than what you should do by writing a, b, or c on your paper. *be honest.*

1. I:
   a. rarely study math every school day.
   b. often study math every school day.
   c. almost always study math every school day.

2. I:
   a. rarely select a study buddy to help me in math.
   b. often select a study buddy to help me in math.
   c. almost always select a study buddy to help me inmath.

3. I:
   a. rarely become anxious and forget important concepts during a math test.
   b. often become anxious and forget important concepts during a math test.
   c. almost always become anxious and forget important concepts during a math test.

4. I:
   a. rarely study math at least two to four hours a week.
   b. often study math at least two to four hours a week.
   c. almost always study math at least two to four hours a week.

5. Each week, I:
   a. rarely plan the best time to study math.
   b. often plan the best time to study math.
   c. almost always plan the best time to study math.

6. I:

    a. rarely use an abbreviation system when taking notes.

    b. often use an abbreviation system when taking notes.

    c. almost always use an abbreviation system when taking notes.

7. When I take math notes, I:

    a. rarely copy all the steps to a problem.

    b. often copy all the steps to a problem.

    c. almost always copy all the steps to a problem.

8. When I become confused in math class, I:

    a. rarely stop taking notes.

    b. often stop taking notes.

    c. almost always stop taking notes.

9. I:

    a. rarely fail to ask questions in math class.

    b. often fail to ask questions in math class.

    c. almost always fail to ask question in math class.

10. I:

    a. rarely stop reading the math textbook when I get stuck.

    b. often stop reading the math textbook when I get stuck.

    c. almost always stop reading the math textbook when I get stuck.

11. When I have difficulty understanding the math topic, I:

    a. rarely go to the instructor or tutor.

    b. often go to the instructor or tutor.

    c. almost always go to the instructor or tutor.

12. I:

    a. rarely review class notes or read the textbook assignment before doing my homework.

    b. often review class notes or read the textbook assignment before doing my homework.

    c. almost always review class notes or read the textbook assignment before doing my homework.

13. I:

    a. rarely fall behind in completing math homework assignments.

    b. often fall behind in completing math homework assignments.

    c. almost always fall behind in completing math homework assignments.

14. After reading the math textbook, I:

    a. rarely mentally review what I have read.

    b. often mentally review what I have read.

    c. almost always mentally review what I have read.

15. There:

    a. rarely are distractions that bother me when I study.

    b. often are distractions that bother me when I study.

    c. almost always are distractions that bother me when I study.

16. I:

    a. rarely do most of my studying the night before the test.

    b. often do most of my studying the night before the test.

    c. almost always do most of my studying the night before the test.

17. I:

    a. rarely develop memory techniques to remember math concepts.

    b. often develop memory techniques to remember math concepts.

    c. almost always develop memory techniques to remember math concepts.

18. When taking a math test, I:

    a. rarely start on the first problem and work the remaining problems in their numbered order.

    b. often start on the first problem and work the remaining problems in their numbered order.

    c. almost always start on the first problem and work the remaining problems in their numbered order.

19. Even when time permits, I:

    a. rarely check over my test answers.

    b. often check over my test answers.

    c. almost always check over my test answers.

20. When my math test is returned, I:

    a. rarely analyze the test errors.

    b. often analyze the test errors.

    c. almost always analyze the test errors.

MATH TEST SCORING
FOR STUDY SKILLS

On a separate sheet of paper put the point value for each answer. The order of the items are different for Section A and Section B. To the right of each item's score are page numbers where the information on this topic is discussed in the book. Put these page numbers by your answer for each question. For immediate help read the reference pages on the items you received one point.

SECTION A POINT VALUE EACH STATEMENT

Items	Answer A (1 point)	Answer B (3 points)	Answer C (5 points)	Book Reference
1.	_____	_____	_____	pp. 23, 68
2.	_____	_____	_____	pp. 26
4.	_____	_____	_____	pp. 63 - 67
5.	_____	_____	_____	pp. 68 - 69, 116
6.	_____	_____	_____	pp. 86 - 87
7.	_____	_____	_____	pp. 92 - 93
11.	_____	_____	_____	pp. 100 - 101
12.	_____	_____	_____	pp. 102 - 105
14.	_____	_____	_____	pp. 101
17.	_____	_____	_____	pp. 126 - 129
19.	_____	_____	_____	pp. 139
20.	_____	_____	_____	pp. 140 - 144

TOTAL _____ + _____ + _____ = _____

SECTION A

SECTION B POINT VALUE EACH STATEMENT

Items	Answer A (5 point)	Answer B (3 points)	Answer C (1 points)	Book Reference
3.	_____	_____	_____	pp. 75
8.	_____	_____	_____	pp. 86, 88 - 90
9.	_____	_____	_____	pp. 91 - 92
10.	_____	_____	_____	pp. 99 - 100
13.	_____	_____	_____	pp. 104
15.	_____	_____	_____	pp. 114 - 115
16.	_____	_____	_____	pp. 117 - 118
18.	_____	_____	_____	pp. 137 - 139

TOTAL _____ + _____ + _____ = _____

SECTION B

_____ + _____ = _____

SECTION A   SECTION B   GRAND TOTAL

A score of 70 or below means you have poor math study skills.

A score between 70 and 90 means that you have good study skills, but you can improve.

A score above 90 means that you have excellent math study skills.

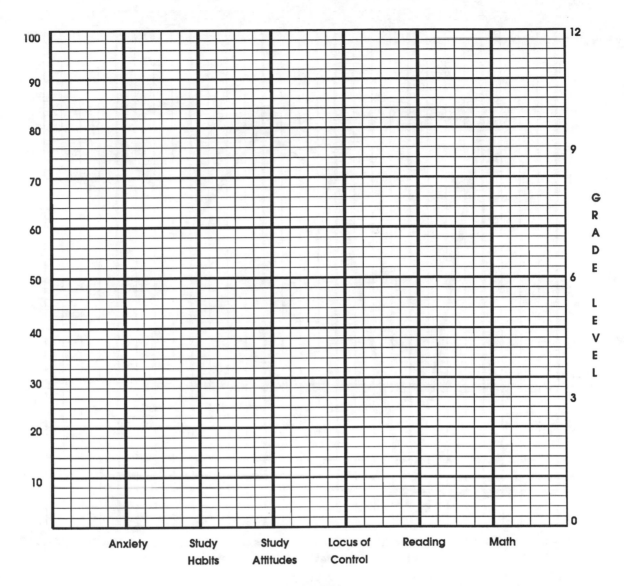

Figure 2
Student Profile Sheet

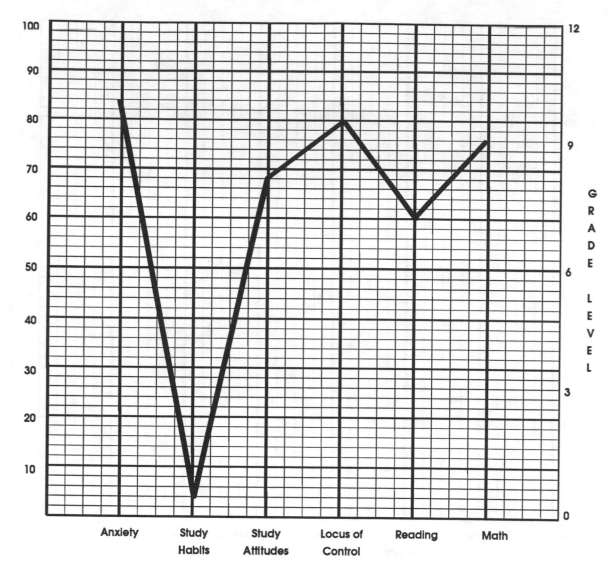

Figure 3
Student Profile Sheet

Figure 3 represents the profile of a high school junior who works part time. She has extremely high mathematics anxiety, poor study habits, good study attitudes, internal locus of control, average reading level and about an eighth grade mathematics level.

This student must learn how to decrease her mathematics anxiety and improve her study skills. Because of her good attitude about school and her average reading level and mathematics level she has the potential of being a very successful math student.

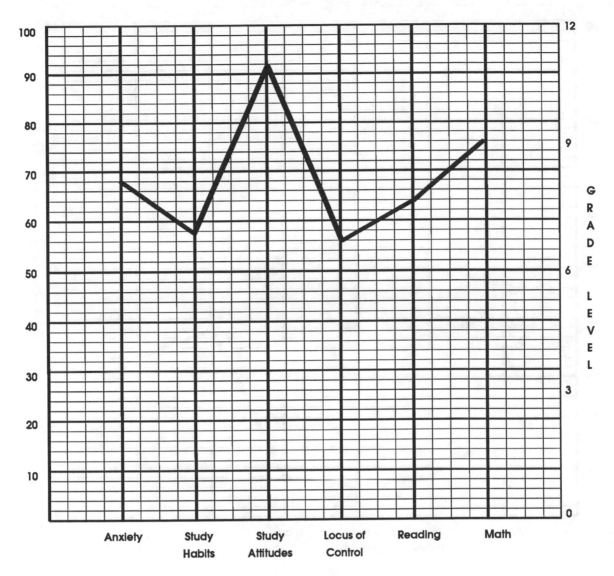

Figure 4
Student Profile Sheet

Figure 4 represents a profile of a junior in high school who has moderate test anxiety, average study habits and excellent study attitude. The students locus of control and reading ability are average, while she has a eighth grade math level. Her problem with passing math is similar to the student's profile in Figure 3, though not as drastic. However, the student in Figure 4 still has to decrease her test anxiety, improve her study habits, and become more internal in order to be successful in math.

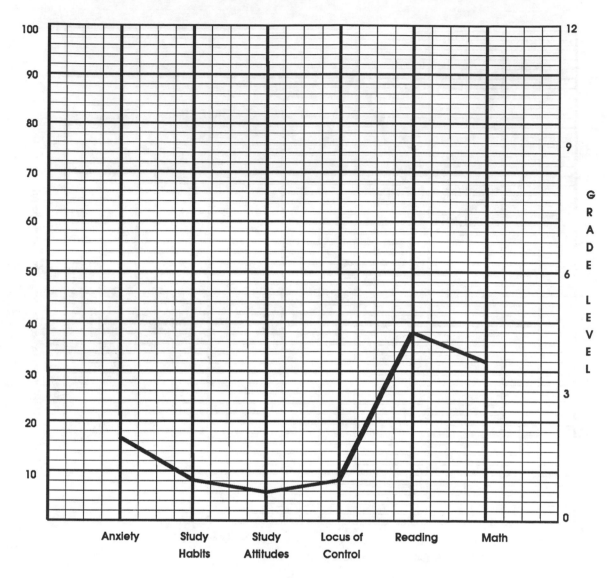

Figure 5
Student Profile Sheet

Figure 5 represents a sophomore who had a long history of failing math. The only two positive characteristics of this student are her low test anxiety and average reading level. She has very poor study habits, poor study attitude, and is external in her locus of control - all probably due to not being successful and failing math so many times. Her reading skills during elementary and middle school are average. Her math skills are low. This external student must believe she can pass math through improving her study habits and attitudes. She also needs support from her teacher and counselor to become more internal and pass math.

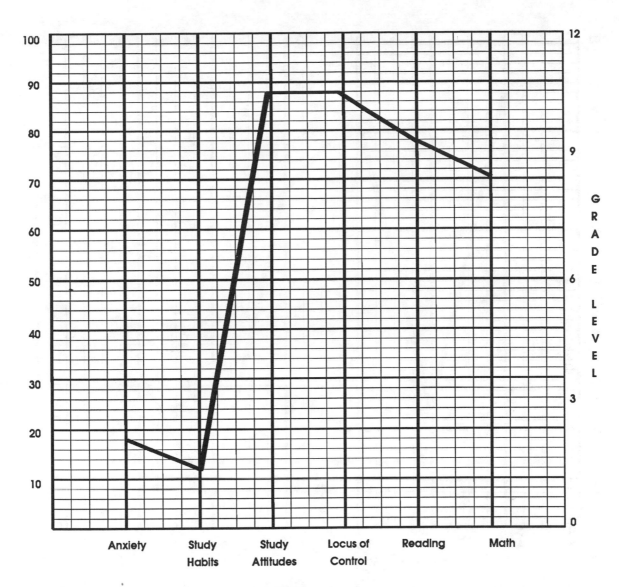

Figure 6
Student Profile Sheet

Figure 6 represents a ninth grader who has low anxiety, excellent study attitude, excellent reading level and an internal locus of control. His math level is average. It appears that his poor study habits are the major block to becoming successful in math.

His poor study habits consist of poor note taking and doing math homework once a week. To pass the remaining high school math course he needs to study math and do his homework every day. He needs to improve his memory skills and test- taking skills.

This "C" student has the potential of becoming an "A" student.

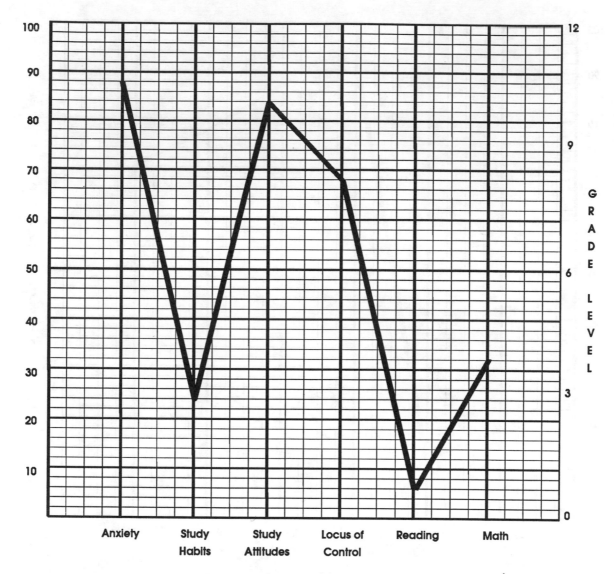

Figure 7
Student Profile Sheet

Figure 7 is the profile of an eighth grader who has below average study habits and above average locus of control. His test anxiety is high but his study attitudes are very good. His poor reading level may indicate a learning problem. His math level is below average. High test anxiety can cause problems during tests and while doing homework. His low reading level is the major block in learning math word problems.

To reduce test anxiety and to be successful in school, this student may need special help or tutoring in reading and math.

SUMMARY

The three major areas that contribute to a student's grade are intelligence and entry level skills, quality of instruction and a student's personal characteristics.

Mathematics success is primarily based on improving the characteristics that affect your ability to learn math - your personal learning characteristics. The major personal learning characteristics are study habits, anxiety, test- taking and control over mathematics.

There are various ways to improve you entry skills and quality of instruction. Once you are placed in the right mathematics course, success is based on your ability to learn math. Understanding which personal learning characteristics you need to improve may be done by identifying your strengths and weaknesses.

HOMEWORK EXERCISES

1. List some factors that determine success in mathematics.

2. Bloom's research shows three areas contribute to success in mathematics. List these three areas and the percent of the grade accounted for by each of these areas.

3. Give at least one definition of intelligence (I.Q.).

4. What are entry level skills?

5. What does quality of instruction mean?

6. What characteristics are included in a students personal characteristics?

7. Why are entry level skills important?

8. What are three ways that entry level skills can be improved?

9. What is the best way to review your last math course? List additional ways.

10. Doing your math homework in a notebook is desirable. Explain why.

11. Why is it a good idea to save your math tests?

12. Explain why tutoring does not always have to be expensive.

13. Who is your best tutor?

14. If your teacher is not available for extra help as often as you need it and can not tutor you professionally, who might give you some names of professional tutors?

15. What would be a good time to discuss with your teacher items like class rules, grading policies , etc?

16. a) Of the three major areas that affect your grade,which one do you have the most control over?
    b) What percent of your grade (according to Bloom) is affected by this area?

17. Name one positive and one negative mathematics learningcharacteristic.

18. Name five standardized tests that are used to determine academic strengths and weaknesses.

19. There are 5 sample student profiles found at the end of this chapter. What is the purpose of studying those profiles?

20. Complete the math study skills evaluation found at the end of this chapter. (Be sure not to write in this book.) Remember to indicate what you actually do rather than what you should do.

21. Name five symptoms of test anxiety as listed in this chapter. List any other symptoms that you know.

22. What effect does too much test anxiety have on your grade?

Notes:

CHAPTER 4
Budgeting Your Time

4

One of the main problems students have is managing their time. In the middle and high school grades, school time is managed by teachers and counselors. Usually after-school hours are managed by the student. There is only so much time for homework, sports, television, social, work and other activities.

The number of high school students working has increased. Students sometimes work to midnight, then have to go to school the next day. Many of these students are working to support their car, to buy nice clothes or to have date money.

When students are asked their number one reason for poor grades they indicate they do not have enough time to study. When students are asked how much time they study per week, most do not have any idea. However, these students know how many hours they work per week and the amount of their pay check. *Students who do not set aside study time may fail mathematics.*

Developing a Study Schedule

There are two basic reasons for developing a study schedule. *The first reason is to set aside a certain amount of study time per day and per week.* Mathematics should be studied every day, while other courses may be studied once or twice per week.

How many hours do you study per week? Five hours, ten hours, fifteen hours, twenty hours? Without knowing the amount of your study hours per week, you will not know if you are studying enough. If you want to make a "B" average, and with studying ten hours a week you make all "B's" on your tests, then you have studied enough. However, if you study five hours a week and make all "D's", then you need to increase your study time. Keep track of your grades and weekly hours studied. Then, you can change your study schedule to get the grades you want.

The second reason for developing a study schedule is efficiency. Efficient study means knowing the best time to study and the worst time to study. This means you won't be thinking about other things when you sit down to study.

The opposite is also true. When doing other things you will not feel guilty about not studying. This is a problem that most students think other students do not have.

FOR EXAMPLE, you are at the mall on a Saturday afternoon having a good time. Then, you start feeling guilty. You have not started studying for that mathematics test on Monday. By having a study schedule you can arrange to study for the mathematics test on Sunday and be with your friends on Saturday.

A study schedule is set up for two reasons:

1. To figure the amount of study time you need per week and per day to get the grades you want.
2. To set up the best study times.

Budgeting Your Daily Time

To develop a study schedule, find the Planning Use of Your Daily Time (see Figure 8) and review it. Use the Planning Use of Your Daily Time as your study schedule. The best way to develop your study schedule is to begin by filling in all the times you can not study.

Step 1 - Block out the hours you are at school, identifying by code C (class). For example, if you are in school from eight to three, put code C in the 8:00 box and draw a line down the center of the column to the 3:00 box on the study schedule. Make sure you do not include study hall and lunch time.

Step 2 - Fill in the time it takes you to get to and from school, either by school bus or private automobile, using code T (transportation).

Step 3 - If you have a job outside your home, fill in the time you work, using code W (work). This may be difficult if your work schedule changes week to week, but put down the times as best you can. As your work hours change, change your study schedule times. REMEMBER: The study schedule is for looking at the number of hours a week you plan to study. Understand that your work time might change every week but your total weekly work hours usually remain the same.

Step 4 - Decide the amount of time it takes to eat. This includes food preparation and

"PLANNING USE OF DAILY TIME"

cleanup if these are your chores. In the study schedule place code E (eat) for the approximate time you use eating breakfast and dinner. Include lunch times on weekends.

Step 5 - Include your personal hygiene time. Personal hygiene includes taking a bath, washing your hair, and other activities that are required to get ready for school, dates, etc. Do not forget the time required to get cleaned up after athletic activities. Personal hygiene can vary from minutes to hours a day for different students. Put code PH (personal hygiene) in the study schedule for the amount of time you spend per week. Remember that more time may be spent on personal hygiene during weekends.

Step 6 - Reserve time for family activities. This may include going to a younger brother's soccer game, teaching a younger sister the newest cheers, visiting grandparents, playing cards with family members or attending church. Use code FA (family activities) on your study schedule.

Step 7 - Figure out how much time is spent on home chores. This time may include cleaning your room, car or clothes, mowing the lawn or taking out the garbage. Put this time on the study schedule using code HC (home chores).

Figure 8
Planning Use of Your Daily Time
Master Plan

	7:00	8:00	9:00	10:00	11:00	12:00	1:00	2:00	3:00	4:00	5:00	6:00	7:00	8:00	9:00	10:00	11:00	12:00
Monday																		
Tuesday																			
Wednesday																			
Thursday																			
Friday																			
Saturday																			
Sunday																			

Step 8 - Review your sleep patterns for the week. Your sleep time will probably be the same from Monday to Friday. On weekends you might sleep later during the day and stay up later at night. If you have been sleeping on Saturday mornings until ten o'clock, do not think it will be easy to study at eight o'clock. Be honest when putting down your sleep time on the study schedule. Use code SL (sleep).

Step 9 - Figure the amount of your weekly social time. Social time includes time spent with your friends or watching television or reading by yourself. Social time can be doing nothing or going out and having a good time. Some students mark off the entire weekend for social time. Code your social time by using SC (social time).

Step 10 - Put down the time spent on activities such as football, track, cheerleading, drama, band, Boy or Girl Scouts, church school committees, etc. Indicate these activities on your study schedule by code A (activities). Time spent on activities may change by semester or season, so revise your study schedule as your activities change.

Now count up all the blank spaces. Each blank space represents one hour. Remember, you might have several half blank spaces that represent a half hour. Take that total number, put it on the upper right hand corner of the study schedule and circle it.

Next, figure how many hours you have to study each day. Then, figure out how many hours you have to study each for the week. Remember, for some courses, like mathematics, daily study is necessary. If you've been receiving C's in math with one hour study each night, it might take an hour and a half or two hours to raise your grade to B. Most students need to study at least ten hours a week to get good grades. Write the amount of time you think you should study per week in the upper left hand corner of your study schedule and put a square around it. This is a study agreement you are making with yourself.

If the number of agreed upon hours are less than the number in the circle, then fill in the times you want to study (S = study). Fill in your best study times first. If there are any unmarked spaces, use them as back up study time. Now you have the best time to study.

On the other hand, if you need to study fifteen hours a week and only have ten hours of space, you must make a decision. Or if you need to study at least two hours each and every school night and only have one hour of space on a few evenings, you have to make a decision.

Go back over your study schedule codes and locate where you can make some changes. If you have a problem locating enough study time, list where your time is used based on how important it is. You will have to decide just what events are more or less important than others. Take away the hours from the items with the least importance. Complete the study schedule by putting in your best study times.

Selecting a Grade as a Course Goal

Decide what grade you want to make in your math course. This should be an "A", "B" or "C". Do not indicate "D" or "F". "F" is a failing grade. "D" means you might not pass the next math course. Write the grade you pick on your study schedule. *This is your goal.*

You now have a study schedule showing the amount of hours of study per day and per week. You also have a course grade goal.

After being in your math class several weeks, you will know if you are reaching your goal. If you find that you are not meeting your goal, you will have three choices.

1. You must increase the hours for math study.
2. You must improve the quality of your study.
3. Lower your course grade goal. The third choice does not count if you put "C" as a course goal.

Selecting a Grade Point Average (GPA) Goal

If the grading system in your school uses a Grade Point Average (GPA), write down the grade point average you want for the semester or for the year on your study schedule. Do you want a 4.0 average (all "A's"), a 3.0 average ("B's"), a 2.5 average ("B's" and "C's") or a 2.0 average (all "C's")? If you have a 5.0 grading system, then adjust the GPA to that scale.

Do not pick an average below 2.0. This indicates below average achievement, though you may be able to graduate with a 1.5 GPA. Be realistic in deciding an overall grade point average.

Developing an Effective Study Plan for the Week

Lastly, develop an effective study plan for the next week. Then, every Sunday, develop a plan to best use your study time for the following week. Most importantly, decide the best time to study math. *Math must be studied every school day.*

Write your weekly study goals on the Weekly Study Goal Sheet (Figure 9). First, write down when you will study math for the next week, then fill in the remaining study time with your other subjects. Planning ahead becomes very important during test or exam times and at the end of each grading period.

Figure 9
Weekly Study Goal Sheet

Subjects	Mon.	Tues.	Weds.	Thurs.	Fri.	Sat.	Sun.
Math course							

SUMMARY

You have now completed a study schedule and Weekly Study Goal Sheet. These schedules indicate the times to study and the amount of study hours per day and per week. The amount of study hours you agreed upon with yourself can change based on the grades you want and the grades you receive.

You may change your math course grade goal from "C" to "B". This may require more study time.

If you do not receive your course grade goal, you can increase your study time and/or improve the quality of your studying.

Taking control over your study time can greatly improve your grades.

HOMEWORK EXERCISES

1. What is one of the main problems students have regarding their study?

2. What reason do students give most for poor grades?

3. What is the danger to students who do not budget their time?

4. What are the two basic reasons for developing a study schedule?

5. Does mathematics have to be studied every day?

6. Explain why you think it is important to save a certain amount of time each day for study.

7. a) How many hours do you study math each week?
   b) Are you satisfied with your present math grade?
   c) Do you think there is a relationship between how much time you study math and your math grade? (Why or why not?)

8. What does efficient study mean?

9. a) Review the <u>Planning Use of Your Daily Time</u> form and make a copy of the form.

   b) Using steps 1 - 10 and the additional directions found in this chapter, complete the <u>Planning Use of Your Daily Time</u> form.

10. If you need to study 2 hours each night, but do not have any spaces left in your <u>Planning Use of Your Daily Time</u> form, what should you do?

11. What should you do if you find you are not getting the grades that you wanted?

12. What would your grade point average (GPA) be if you earned grades of A, B, A, B, C, C. Use A = 4, B = 3, C = 2, D = 1.

(Optional Question)

13*. a) Review the <u>Weekly Study Goal Sheet</u> and make a copy of it.

   b) Complete the <u>Weekly Study Goal Sheet</u>.

*NOTE:

   1. Question 13 should be done after question 9 has been completed.
   2. Questions 9 and 13 will take extra time to complete (some class time might be appropriate).

CHAPTER 5
Math Anxiety and How to Reduce It

5

Test anxiety is not new. It has existed for as long as tests have been used to determine students' grades. Over the past forty-five years, studies have shown that high test anxiety *does* influence grades. It leads to low test scores.

At the University of South Florida, Dr. Charles Spielberger studied the similarity between test anxiety and how smart your are. The results were very interesting. They suggest that if you are very smart, then anxiety may actually improve your performance. But if you are as smart as the average student, then anxiety can cause poor performance.

ANXIETY + BEING SMART = IMPROVEMENT

ANXIETY + AVERAGE SMARTNESS = NO IMPROVEMENT

His findings showed that students of average smartness with low test anxiety had higher grades than students of average smartness with high test anxiety.

Test anxiety is a learned response. That means you were not born with it. It does not "come naturally". It can lead to stress that in time can lead to physical and psychological problems.

Defining Test Anxiety

There are several definitions of test anxiety. One definition states, "Test anxiety is a conditional emotional habit to either a single terrifying experience, recurring experience of high anxiety or a continuous condition of anxiety." This definition sounds complicated. But what it means is that a person is not born with test anxiety.

A situation in one's life can cause test anxiety. This situation can happen all at once or it may take several tests to cause test anxiety. *Test anxiety is a learned response that can be unlearned.*

Another definition of test anxiety is related to the school system. This definition suggests that test anxiety is the expectation of some realistic or non-realistic threat. The "threatening situation" may be an actual test or it may be in the form of an oral report, a written report, work at the board or a science project.

Learning the Causes of Test Anxiety

The causes of test anxiety can be different for each student. These causes may be explained by four basic concepts.

1. Test anxiety can be a learned behavior resulting from the expectations of parents, teachers or other important people in the student's life.
2. Test anxiety can be caused by student's thinking that grades are related to how they think about themselves.
3. Test anxiety develops from fear of losing friends due to poor grades, or upsetting parents or family.
4. Test anxiety can result from a feeling of lack of control or from a feeling of being unable to change one's life.

Mathematics test anxiety is a new idea in education. It was first presented to the general public in 1976 when Ms. magazine published: "Math Anxiety: Why is a Smart Girl Like You Counting on Your Fingers?" About that same time, some educators began using the term *mathophobia* as a cause for children's unwillingness to learn mathematics. Other studies discovered mathematics anxiety was also common among adults. Until that time, however, educators had thought of math anxiety only as a problem in doing math. We now believe that to be wrong.

There are several definitions of math anxiety:

* Math anxiety is having a very negative attitude towards mathematics.
* Math anxiety is the feeling of tension and anxiety when you work with numbers and try to solve math problems in a test situation.
* Math anxiety is the state of panic, helplessness, and mental confusion that occurs when you have to solve mathematical problems.

There are two types of mathematical anxiety:

* Math test anxiety.
* Numerical anxiety.

Math test anxiety involves thinking about the test, finishing the test and getting the grade back. Numerical anxiety refers to everyday situations that require working with numbers.

Math anxiety exists among many students who do not have problems in other courses. It occurs often in middle school and high school students, more so in girls than boys. These students usually had poor math backgrounds in elementary school. Educators studying anxiety and mathematics grades have shown that anxiety is one reason for poor grades in math, especially among girls. Educators also have shown that reducing math test anxiety *does not* mean higher math grades. *Students must also have good math study skills to learn the math material and to be good test-takers.*

"REDUCING TEST ANXIETY"

Reducing Test Anxiety

To reduce mathematics test anxiety, an understanding of the relaxation response is required. The relaxation response is any technique or method that helps you to become more relaxed. It will take the place of an anxiety response.

The two basic types of test anxiety controlled by the relaxation response are physical and mental anxiety. Physical anxiety occurs in your body. Signs of physical anxiety are upset stomach, sweaty palms, pains in the neck, or general feelings of nervousness. These feelings of nervousness prevent you from concentrating on the test. Mental anxiety is negative self-talk that distracts you from concentrating on the test.

FOR EXAMPLE, during a test you keep telling yourself, "I can not do it. I can not do the problems, and I am going to fail this test." The more you tell yourself that you will fail, the less time you spend working on the test.

There are short- and long-term relaxation response procedures that help control mathematics test anxiety. Effective short-term techniques include the tensing and differential relaxation method, and the palming method.

The tensing and differential relaxation method helps you relax by tensing and relaxing your muscles all at once. Follow these procedures, while you are sitting at your desk and before taking a test:

1. Put your feet flat on the floor.
2. With your hands, grab under the chair.
3. Push down with your feet and pull up on your chair at the same time for about five seconds.
4. Relax for five to ten seconds.
5. Repeat two-three times.
6. Relax all your muscles except the ones that are actually used to take the test.

The palming method is a visualization procedure used to reduce test anxiety. Visualization procedures are similar to day dreaming. While you are at your desk before or during a test, follow these procedures:

1. Close your eyes and cover them using the center of the palms of your hands.
2. Prevent your hands from touching your eyes by resting the lower parts of the

palms on your cheekbones and placing your fingers on your forehead. The eyeballs must not be touched, rubbed or handled in any way.

3. Think of some real or imaginary relaxing scene. This scene could be walking on the beach, walking in the woods, hearing rain hit the roof or watching the sun set. Mentally visualize this scene. Picture the scene as if you were actually there, looking through your own eyes.

4. Visualize this relaxing scene for one to two minutes. Practice visualizing this scene several days before taking a test and the effectiveness of this relaxation procedure will improve.

The audio cassette, How To Reduce Test Anxiety (Side One) further explains test anxiety and discusses these and other short-term relaxation response techniques. These short-term relaxation techniques can be learned quickly but are not as successful as the long-term relaxation technique. Short-term techniques are intended to be used while learning the long- term technique.

The cue-controlled relaxation response technique is the best long-term relaxation technique. It is presented on "Side Two" of the audio cassette, How To Reduce Test Anxiety. Cue-controlled relaxation means you can start your own relaxation based on repeating certain cue words to yourself. It is similar to hearing an old song on the radio and having your feelings change. You are taught to relax and then silently repeat cue words such as "I am relaxed." After enough practice you can reduce the amount of time you listen to the tape from twenty-five minutes to two to three minutes. Then, you can repeat the words, "I am relaxed," to yourself and be relaxed. The cue-oriented relaxation techniques have worked with hundreds of students.

For a better understanding of test anxiety and how to reduce it, listen to How To Reduce Test Anxiety (available from the Academic Success Press, Inc., P.O. Box 2567, Pompano Beach, Florida 33072; tel: (305) 785-2034, $14.95 postpaid).

SUMMARY

Mathematics test anxiety is a learned behavior developed by having physical and/or mental responses during previous tests. *Physical anxiety occurs in the body. Mental anxiety occurs in the mind.*

Mathematics anxiety can decrease your ability to do well on tests and can be overcome by learning cue-controlled relaxation. However, reducing your mathematics test anxiety does not guarantee success on tests. *You must know and remember the right material for a test.*

Your mathematics test anxiety can be greatly reduced by following the instructions presented on the audio cassette tape, How To Reduce Test Anxiety.

HOMEWORK EXERCISES

1. How long has test anxiety existed?

2. Is it true that some anxiety with smart students improves their grades?

3. Is it true that test anxiety is a learned response that can be unlearned?

4. What are the four basic concepts that explain the causes of test anxiety?

5. Give at least two definitions of mathematics anxiety.

6. Is it true that mathematics anxiety occurs more frequently with females rather than males?

7. Is it true that mathematics anxiety occurs more frequently with students having a poor math background?

8. Besides reducing mathematics test anxiety, what else is needed for better understanding and higher grades?

9. What is a relaxation response?

10. State in your own words the two basic types of test anxiety.

11. Describe the two techniques used for short-term relaxation.

12. Name the best long-term relaxation technique.

CHAPTER 6

Improving Your Listening Skill and Learning to Take Good Notes

6

Nearly a third of your school age years are spent in the classroom. To avoid wasting these valuable years, GET THE MOST OUT OF YOUR CLASS TIME. This is accomplished by developing good study skills in the classroom. Good classroom study skills involve learning to be a good listener and developing good note-taking techniques.

Being a Good Listener

Has anyone ever told you that you are a good listener? That's a very nice compliment. But listening takes skill, especially in the classroom.

Some students think that listening means hearing. But listening means hearing AND trying to understand what was said.

Being a good listener is a skill that can be learned. Pay special attention to the next section on effective listening in the classroom.

Effective Listening

Becoming an effective listener is an important skill and is the basis for good note taking. Effective listening can be learned through a set of skills you can practice. To become an effective listener you must prepare yourself with your body and mind.

The body preparation in becoming an effective listener involves where you sit in the classroom. Sit in the best area to obtain high grades: **The Golden Triangle of Success.**

The Golden Triangle of Success begins with seats in the front row and converges to the middle seat in the back row facing the teacher's desk (See Figure 10). Students sitting in this area directly face the teacher and have to pay attention in class. Also, there is less chance for

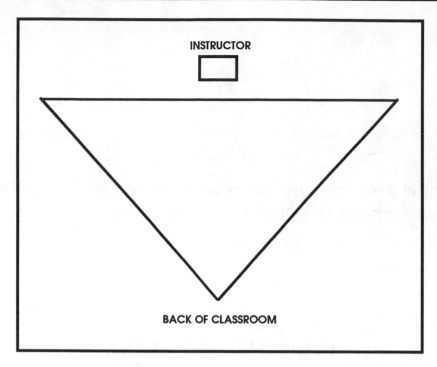

INSTRUCTOR

BACK OF CLASSROOM

Figure 10
The Golden Triangle of Success

these students to be bothered by students outside the classroom or by students making noise within the classroom.

When you're located in The Golden Triangle you can hear the teacher better. The teacher's voice is pointed to the middle seat in the back row. This means there is less chance of not understanding the teacher and you can hear well enough to ask good questions. Thus, by sitting in **The Golden Triangle of Success,** you can make yourself pay more attention during class. Also, you will be less distracted by other students. This is very important for math students, since math teachers usually go over a point once and continue on to the next point. If you miss that point in the lesson, then you could be "lost" for the rest of the class.

Mind preparation for note taking involves *warming up* before class begins and *becoming an active listener*. Just like an football player must *warm up* before a game begins, you must warm up before taking notes. Warm up by:

* reviewing the last day's notes

* reviewing the reading material

* reviewing the homework, or by

* making up questions for the teacher.

This mental warm up of the mind before class allows you to refresh your memory and prepare important questions. This makes it easier to learn new material.

Becoming an active listener is the second part of mind preparation for note taking. Some ways to become an active listener include looking at the teacher and listening for main ideas. You can also nod your head or say to yourself, "I understand," when agreeing with the teacher.

Do not guess what the teacher is going to say or judge too fast the teacher's information before the point is made. Jumping to conclusions will cause you problems. Listen and learn the information being given to you.

Use your time looking for interesting topics in the lesson. When the teacher talks about information that you need to know, as fast as you can, repeat it to yourself. This will begin the learning process while you are still in the classroom.

REMEMBER: Class time is an important study period that should not be wasted.

Learning Good Note-Taking Techniques

To become a good note taker takes understanding two basic ideas:
1. Be exact in detail. Copy problems down step-by-step.
2. Understand the general principles, general concepts, and general rules.

While taking math notes, you need to copy each and every step of the problem, even though you may know every step of the problem. In the classroom you might understand each step, but a week from now you might not remember how to do the problem. That is why you do need to write all of the steps in your notes. In addition, as each step is written down, it is being memorized. Make sure to copy every step for each problem written on the board.

There will be times in class when you get lost while listening. You should keep taking notes, though you do not understand the problem.

Put a question mark by those steps you do not understand. After class, go over the steps you did not understand with your teacher or with a fellow student.

The goal of note taking is to take the least amount of notes and get the most amount down. This could be the opposite of what some teachers have told you.

Some teachers tell you to write everything down. This is not a good note taking system.

It is very difficult to take good specific notes and hear what the teacher is saying at the same time.

What you need to develop is a note taking system. You need to write the least amount possible and get the most amount down on paper, while still hearing what the teacher is saying.

Developing Abbreviations

To reduce the amount of written notes, an abbreviation system is needed.

FOR EXAMPLE: When the teacher starts explaining a math idea such as least common denominator you need to write it out the first time. After that, use "LCD". You need to develop abbreviations for all the most commonly used words in mathematics.

Figure 11 has a list of some common abbreviations. Add your own abbreviations to this list. By using abbreviations as much as possible, you can obtain the same meaning from your notes. Then, you will have more time to listen to the teacher.

Using the Modified Two-Column System

Another procedure to save time while taking notes is to stop writing complete sentences. Write your main thoughts in phrases. Phrases are easier to put down and easier to memorize.

One of the best math note taking systems is the modified two column system (See Figures 12 and 13). This note taking system divides the note page into three columns. The first column is the margin to the left of the red line and is used for putting down key ideas and key words. Key words or key ideas represent the main points of the lecture such as add fractions, important formulas, associative property rules, etc. If possible, write down the key words and key ideas during the lecture.

The next note taking section is *Discussion of Rules*. In this section, write down and explain the important arithmetic or algebra rules that apply to the problem. Also, add any other important notes by writing short phrases and abbreviations. Put question marks by the material which is not understood.

The example column in the note system (far right) is for writing out the problems. Each problem written on the board or discussed in class should be written down step-by- step. If you

SYMBOL	MEANING	SYMBOL	MEANING
ie	For Example	(Quadratic)	Circle words you do not understand and need to look up
∴	Therefore	?	Do not understand
∵	Because	1 2 3	To indicate a series of facts
∈	Belongs To	et. al.	And Others
∋	Such That	etc	And So Forth
∠	Angle	ref	Reference
△	Triangle	*	Important
▢	Square	bk	Book
○	Circle	pg	Page
→	Implies	N.B.	Note Well, Important
>	Greater Than	NO	Shows Disagreement
<	Less Than (Note difference from angle symbol)	com	Commutative
=	Equal To	asc	Associative
two times a number	Underline a sentence to indicate an important idea	dst	Distributive

Figure 11
Abbreviations

get confused by a step, then put a question mark by it for additional study. If you can, put down a page number from the textbook by the examples.

KEY IDEAS WORDS	DISCUSSION OF RULES NOTES	EXAMPLES
Add Fractions	Need a least common denominator	$\dfrac{1}{3} + \dfrac{3}{4}$
	L.C.D. is 12	
	Multiply each fraction by one	$\dfrac{1}{3} \cdot \dfrac{4}{4} + \dfrac{3}{4} \cdot \dfrac{3}{3}$
	Simplify Fractions	$\dfrac{4}{12} + \dfrac{9}{12}$
	Add	$\dfrac{13}{12}$ or $1\dfrac{1}{12}$

Figure 12
Modified Two-Column System

Knowing When and When Not to Take Notes

To become a better note taker, you need to know when to take notes and when not to take notes. The teacher will give tips that will tell you what material is important. Here are some tips:

* facts or ideas listed or emphasized
* writing on the board and underlining or circling words or phrases
* saying that certain problems will be on the test

KEY IDEAS WORDS	DISCUSSION OF RULES NOTES	EXAMPLES
Example		$5(W + 3) + 3(W + 1) = 14$
Distributive Property	Multiplication distributes over addition	$5W + 15 + 3W + 3 = 14$
Communative Property	Addends may be in any order	$5W + 3W + 15 + 13 = 14$
Associative Property	Addends may be grouped in any way	$(5W + 3W) + (15 + 3) = 14$
Addition	Addition of Like Terms	$8W + 18 = 14$
Addition	Add -18 to both sides	$8W + 18 - 18 = 14 - 18$
Associative Property	Addends may be grouped in any way	$8W + (18 - 18) = 14 - 18$
Additive Inverse	a number added to its negative is zero	$8W + 0 = 14 - 18$
Property of zero	zero added to any number is that number	$8W = 14 - 18$
Addition		$8W = -4$
Mult. Property	multiply both sides by 1/8	$1/8(8W) = 1/8(-4)$
Multiplication		$W = -4/8$
Simplify	Reduce fraction	$W = -1/2$

Figure 13
Modified Two-column System

* summarizing
* pausing
* repeating statements
* saying "1,2,3" or "A,B,C"
* working several examples of the same type of problem on the blackboard
* when the teacher says, "This is a tricky problem. Most students will miss it."
  For example, 5/0 is undefined, not zero
* when the teacher says, "This is the most difficult step in the problem."

You need to learn the tips your teacher gives about important material. If you are in doubt about the importance of the class material, do not hesitate to ask the teacher.

While taking notes, math material can become confusing. At this point take as many notes as possible. Do not give up on note taking. As you take notes on confusing problem steps, skip lines, then go back and fill in information which helps you understand the steps you do not know. Ask your teacher for help with the uncompleted problem steps. Write down the reasons for each step in the space provided.

Using a Tape Recorder

Having a math teacher who talks too fast for you or not being able to get all the information down presents a problem. If you have this problem, then ask you teacher if you can bring a tape recorder to class. Although some teachers will not want their lessons taped for good reasons, there will be others who will not mind.

To use the tape recorder successfully, the tape recorder must have a tape counter. The tape counter displays a number showing the amount of tape you have listened to. When you find you are in an area you do not understand, write the beginning and ending tape counter number in the left margin of your notes.

When going over your notes, the tape counter number will be a reference point for getting information to work the problem. You can also reduce the time it takes to listen to the tape by using the pause button. This will stop the recording of unnecessary material.

"USING A TAPE RECORDER"

Asking Questions

To obtain the most from a lesson, you must ask questions in class. By asking questions, you improve your understanding of the material and decrease your homework time. By not asking questions, you cause yourself confusion during the rest of the class period. It is easier to ask questions in class about difficult problems in the homework assignment. This will stop you from spending hours trying to figure out the problems on your own.

If you are shy about asking questions in class, then write down the questions and read them to your teacher. If the teacher seems confused about the questions, then talk to the teacher after class. To help yourself to ask questions, remember:

1. You are helping yourself AND your classmates. Other students in class
    have the same question.

2. You will save YOUR homework time by having a better understanding of class material.

3. Your teacher needs comments from the class to help you. Several questions may tell her to slow down.

Recording Each Problem Step

One last suggestion in note taking is to record each step of every problem written or verbally explained. By recording each problem step, you begin overlearning how to work the problems.

This procedure will increase your problem-solving speed during future tests.

Also, if you get stuck on your homework, you will have complete examples to review.

The major reason for this procedure is to understand how to do the problems while the teacher is explaining them. This is easier than trying to remember unwritten steps.

Writing down each step of a problem discussed by the teacher may take some time. But it pays off during homework and test time.

Listening and Learning

Some students think listening to the teacher and taking notes is a waste of valuable time. Students too often sit in class and use a fraction of their learning ability.

Class time should be considered a valuable study period where you can listen, take notes, and learn at the same time.

One way to do this is by memorizing important facts when the teacher is talking about material you already know. Another technique is to repeat back to yourself the important ideas right after the teacher says them.

Using class time to learn mathematics is an efficient learning system.

Reworking Your Notes

The note taking system does not stop when you leave the classroom. As soon as possible after class, rework your notes. You can rework the notes in study hall or as soon as you get home.

REMEMBER: Most forgetting occurs right after learning the material. You need to rework the notes to obtain the most value. Do not wait two weeks to rework your notes. You probably will not understand what you have was written later on.

The following are important steps in reworking your notes:

Step 1 — *Rewrite the material you can not read or will not be able to understand in two weeks*. If you do not rework your notes it will be a major problem. An example is coming across important material that you can not read as you study for a test. Another benefit of rewriting the notes is the learning of new material right away. This is better than taking more time to learn the material a few days later.

Step 2 — *Fill in the gaps*. Most of the time when you are listening to the lesson, you can not write everything down. It is almost impossible to write everything down that is important, even if you know shorthand. Locate the part of your notes which are not finished. Fill in the steps or ideas which were left out. In the future, skip two or three lines in your notebook page for known lesson gaps.

Step 3 — *Add additional key words and ideas in the left hand column*. These key words or ideas were the ones not recorded during class. For example, using Figure 12, you did not know you needed a common denominator to add fractions. Adding LCD under the key words column will help you understand the lesson on fractions. Put additional important key words and ideas in your notes. These are the words that will later improve your understanding of mathematics.

Step 4 — *Review your class notes from the beginning of the chapter*. Once you have finished going over your notes, spend five minutes reviewing important parts of the lesson. Try to summarize these major parts in your mind. Then, put together ideas learned in past lessons plus what you have learned today. This will lead to new and better ideas. Try to apply these new ideas when doing your homework.

SUMMARY

Listening is not just hearing. Listening is hearing AND trying to understand what is said. Being an effective listener is a skill that can be learned. It is the first step to excellent note taking. The effective listener knows where to sit in the classroom and understands good listening techniques.

The goal of note taking is to write the least amount possible to record the most information. This allows you to improve your ability to listen to the lecture and increase your learning chances in the classroom.

Rework your notes as soon as possible after class. If you wait too long to review your notes, then you might not understand them. This means it will be more difficult to learn them later. Reworking your notes will improve your understanding of mathematics — and your grades.

HOMEWORK EXERCISES

1. Approximately what part of your day is spent in school?

2. What are two ways to improve classroom study skills?

3. Listening does not only mean hearing. What else does listening mean?

4. Can students learn to be good listeners?

5. What is the basis for good note taking?

6. What two ways do you prepare yourself to be an effective listener?

7. What does body preparation mean as it applies to effective listening?

8. What is the golden triangle of success and explain its benefits.

9. How do some students get "lost" during a math lesson?

10. What two parts does mind preparation involve as it applies to effective listening?

11. What are the steps used by students to warm up before taking class notes?

12. Why is this warm up important?

13. List some ways to become an active listener?

14. In listening to a lecture, what two things will distract you from learning the material?

15. What two ideas are required for good note-taking?

16. Explain why it is important to copy down each step of a problem from class.

17. Why should you continue to take notes, even if you do not understand a step?

18. What is the goal of note taking?

19. Even though it is important to copy down each step of a problem, should you write down everything your teacher says?

20. a) What system will help reduce the amount of written notes?
    b) Why is this system important?

21. Read and study Figure 11. Copy Figure 11 on your own paper and add any abbreviations that you use in math class.

22. In your own words describe the modified two-column system. What is the heading for the first column? The second column? The third column?

23. List ten tips that your teacher gives you to indicate when material is important. Can you think of any others?

24. What is one option to consider if your math teacher teaches too fast for you?

25. To obtain the most from a lesson, you must ask questions in class. Why?

26. What steps can you take if you are shy about asking questions in class?

27. What are three good reasons for asking questions in class? Can you think of any others?

28. You should record each step of every problem in your notebook. Why?

29. Class time is a valuable study period where you can listen, take notes, and learn at the same time. What are two techniques used to accomplish this?

30. When does most forgetting occur?

31. What should you do as soon as possible after class to overcome forgetting the material?

32. What are the four steps used when reworking your notes?

CHAPTER 7

Some Tips on Reading Your Text and Doing Your Homework

7

Reading a mathematics textbook is more difficult than reading textbooks on other subjects. The process for reading a mathematics textbook is different from the way students are generally taught how to read.

In English class, for example, students are taught to read quickly or skim the material. If you did not understand a word, you were to keep on reading. The reason to keep on reading is to pick up the unknown words and their meaning from the surrounding words and sentences.

This reading technique may work when reading a novel. But using it in your math course will be totally confusing. By skipping some major concept words or bold-print words, you will not understand the math textbook. Also homework will become more difficult. Reading a math textbook takes more time and harder thinking than your other textbooks.

Understanding Reading Material

These are the proper steps for reading a math textbook:

Step 1 — Skim the assigned reading material. Skim the material to get the general idea about the major topics. Read the introduction paragraphs to the chapter and topic headings. Continue the skimming by looking at each bold print word and read each property, definition, rule or formula. Skip the homework sections: You do not want to learn the material at this time. You want to get a total *picture* of the assignment. FOR EXAMPLE: Skimming will allow you to see if problems presented in one chapter section are further explained later on.

Step 2 — As you skim the chapter, circle in pencil the new words that you do not understand. If you do not understand these new words after reading the assignment, then ask your teacher for help. Skimming the reading assignment should only take five to ten minutes. Remember to erase all pencil marks when you understand all the new words.

Step 3 — Put all your concentration into reading. REMEMBER: Reading a mathematics textbook is very difficult. It might take you half an hour to read and understand one page. This is because what an English teacher writes in three pages a math teacher writes in one page. The math teacher uses symbols and formulas instead of long sentences. Do not skip any of the reading assignment.

Step 4 — Some authors will skip steps when doing examples. They think the missing steps are easily understood. Some will even write, "It is clear that..." when skipping steps. But, remember, what is clear to the author may not be so clear to you. So, be sure to write down *each* step for better understanding. Later on, when you go back and review, the steps are already filled in. You will understand how each step is done. Also, by filling in the extra steps, you are starting to over-learn the material. This will help you to better recall the material on future tests.

Step 5 — In pencil, underline or circle additional concepts and words that you do not know. Maybe you circled them the first time while skimming. If you understand them now, erase the pencil marks. If you do not understand the words or concepts, then re-read the page. If you need additional help look them up in the glossary. Try not to read any further until you understand all the words and concepts.

Step 6 — If you do not understand the material, follow these eight steps until you *do* understand the material.

    A: Go back to the previous page and re-read the information to maintain a train of thought.

    B: Read ahead to the next page. Discover if any additional information better explains the misunderstood material.

    C: Locate and review any diagrams, examples or rules that explain the misunderstood material.

    D: Read the misunderstood paragraph(s) several times aloud to better understand their meaning.

E: Refer to your math notes for a better explanation of the misunderstood material.

F: Refer to another math textbook that covers the same material.

G: Define exactly what you do not understand and call your study buddy for help.

H: Ask your math teacher for help in understanding the material.

Step 7 — If you still do not clearly understand some words or concepts, develop your own glossary. Put this n the back of your notebook. You need to have a glossary for each chapter in the math book. Then ask the teacher for a better explanation and put it in your glossary. You should know all the words and concepts in your glossary before taking the test.

Step 8 — After you finish reading each section of your book, recall the most important learned concepts. If you have difficulty recalling the important concepts, write them down in your chapter glossary.

Step 9 — Write several questions in your chapter glossary, especially the material you think may be on the test. Use these questions as a future study check.

Step 10 -- In Summary, be an *active* reader. Doing your part as an active reader will enable you to better understand the material presented in the text book.

Hopefully you will not have to use all these steps when you come across material you do not understand. But by using these reading techniques, you have narrowed down the important material for learning.

You have skimmed the textbook to get an overview of the assignment.

You have carefully read the material and noted important parts.

You then developed a glossary of unknown words or concepts. This further narrows down the material to be learned.

The last step is recalling important concepts and writing down questions for future study.

In summary, the most important study material should be reviewed before doing the homework problems. The glossary has to be learned 100 percent before taking the test.

Establishing Study Period Goals

Before beginning your homework, set up goals for your study period. Do not just do the homework problems.

Ask yourself this question: "What am I going to do tonight to become more successful in math?"

By setting up short-term homework goals and completing them, you will feel more confident about mathematics. This also improves the way you feel about yourself. This helps move you toward becoming a more internally motivated student. You have set goals which you have completed.

Study period goals are set up either on a time-line basis or an item-line basis.

A time-line basis is studying math for a certain amount of time. FOR EXAMPLE: You may want to study math for an hour, then switch to another subject.

An item-line basis is studying math until you have completed a certain number of homework problems. For instance, you might set a goal to study math until you have completed all the odd numbered problems.

Doing Your Homework

Doing your homework can be a chore or it can be fun. Most students try to do their homework problems without any type of preparation. They become confused and stop studying. To improve your homework success, *review the day's notes and the author's examples before starting your homework.*

Most students use their math book only as a source for homework problems. When starting homework, these students open the book to the page where the homework problems are located and start doing homework. These same students find themselves constantly going back to their notes or to the author examples. They are looking to see how similar problems were solved. Can you see how useless this system is? Use your book in the way it was intended to be used. Your book is a valuable resource for you. If it was to be used only for homework, it would be much smaller.

Before starting your homework, read and study your notes and the author's examples. This kind of review will not only mean better use of your time, but it will increase your chances of successfully completing your homework. Remember, to be successful in learning the material and doing homework assignments, first review your notes. Then, study the author examples.

Doing your homework neatly has several benefits. When asking your teacher about homework problems, the teacher will be able to read your problem steps. Your teacher will easily locate the mistakes. Then, you will be shown how to correct the steps without your teacher having to understand your handwriting. Another benefit is that when you review for final exams, you can quickly re-learn the homework material. A third benefit is that it takes more concentration to write neatly. More concentration leads to quicker learning of the material. Neatly prepared homework can help you now and in the future.

When doing your homework write down every step of a problem. Even if you can do the step in your head, write it down anyway. This will increase the amount of homework time. But you are over-learning how to solve problems. This improves your memory. By doing every step, you can memorize and understand the material. Another advantage is when you re-work problems that you did wrong. Now it is easy to review each step to find your mistakes. In the long run, *doing every step of the homework will save you time and frustration.*

While doing homework, do not get into the bad habit of memorizing how to do problems without knowing the reasons for each step. Many students are smart enough to memorize procedures needed to complete a set of homework problems. However, when similar homework problems are presented on a test, the student can not solve the problems. To avoid this kind of trouble, keep reminding yourself about the rules, laws, or properties used to solve problems. Here is an example.

$$\text{Add} \qquad \frac{2}{5} + \frac{1}{3}$$

$$\text{Step \#1} \qquad \frac{2}{5} \cdot \frac{3}{3} + \frac{1}{3} \cdot \frac{5}{5}$$

$$\text{Step \#2} \qquad \frac{6}{15} + \frac{5}{15}$$

$$\text{Step \#3} \qquad \frac{11}{15} \qquad \text{Answer}$$

What allows you to multiply 2/5 by 3/3 and 1/3 by 5/5?

Answer: the multiplication property of 1.

Once you know the correct reason for going from one step to another in solving a math problem, then you can answer any problem requiring that property. *Students who memorize how to do problems — instead of understanding the reasons for correctly working the steps — will eventually fail their math course.*

If you get stuck on a homework problem — several things can be done.

Step 1 — Review the textbook or lesson notes which are similar to the problem.

Step 2 — Get another math book or some computer software that will explain how to do the problem.

Step 3 — Call your study buddy.

Step 4 — Skip the problem and get your math teacher to help you.

No matter what homework system you use, remember this important rule: *Always finish a homework session by understanding a concept or doing a homework problem correctly.*

Do not end a homework session with a problem you can not complete. You will lose confidence. All you will think about is the last problem you could not solve, instead of the twenty problems you did solve correctly. If you did quit on a problem you could not solve, return and re-work problems you have done correctly. *Do not end your study period with a problem you could not complete.*

After finishing your homework assignment, recall to yourself or write down the most important learned concepts. This reinforces your ability to do math.

Getting behind in mathematics homework is academic suicide. This means that you will fail your math course!

As mentioned in Chapter One, math is sequential. If you get behind in math, it will be difficult for you to catch up. Each topic builds on the next. It will be like going to Spanish class without learning the last set of vocabulary words. The teacher will be talking to you, using the new vocabulary, but you will not understand what is being said.

After completing your homework problems, a good learning technique is to make note cards. Note cards are 3" X 5" index cards which contain information that is difficult to learn or material you think will be on the test.

On the front of the note card write a math problem or information that you need to know. On the back of the note card write how to work the problem or an explanation of important information.

FOR EXAMPLE: Suppose you are having difficulty remembering that you need a common denominator when adding fractions. Then, you would write some examples on adding fractions on the front of the note card with the answers on the back.

In this way, you can look at the front of the card, repeat to yourself the answer, and check yourself with the back of the card. Make note cards on important information you might forget. Every time you have five spare minutes, pull out your note cards and review them.

To keep up with your math homework, it is necessary to complete your homework every school day. If you have to get behind in one of your courses, make sure it is not math. If you do fall behind in another course, be sure the course is not sequential. This means that knowing one homework assignment does not depend on learning the next homework assignment.

REMEMBER: *Getting behind in math is the fastest way to fail the course.*

Solving Story Problems

The most difficult homework assignment for many math students is solving story/word problems. This is true whether you are in middle school or high school. One of the most important things to realize, however, is that solving story problems is a skill that can be learned. You must keep the following in mind:

1. All story problems have two main parts. One part, usually mentioned first, gives the information required for the solution. The second part asks a question.

2. You must always determine what the question is and then find a way to answer the question.

To solve story problems you must approach your work in an organized manner. The following list will be helpful:

1. Read the problem enough times, so that you can tell the difference between

"SOLVING WORD PROBLEMS"

the given information and the question being asked. Enough times might mean twice for one story problem but five or six times for another. Most students usually skip this step, *but it is very important*.

2. Cross out any information you do not need to solve the problem.

3. You must now begin to make a transition from the words in the story problem to numbers or letters and operations (+, -, x, -). This is done by trying to draw

a picture or a diagram representing the story problem. FOR EXAMPLE: If the story problem is about finding the dimensions of a rectangle, then draw a rectangle. If the problem is about distance, you can use an arrow representing distance, etc.

4. Depending on the story problem, use of a table might be helpful. FOR EXAMPLE: If the problem is about distance, rate and time, a three space table would be helpful. The first space could be labeled distance. The second space could be labeled time and the third space rate. If the story problem asks for distance, for example, fill in numbers for rate and time from the given information. By remembering the formula, **Distance equals Rate times Time,** the table would help you find the distance.

5. You must now write a math statement that can be used to solve the story problem. FOR EXAMPLE: In a distance, rate, time problem where the rate and time are given, the statement might be $D = 60 \times 3$. If you are in an algebra class this step would involve writing an equation.

6. Next you need to solve the mathematics statement (in algebra, the equation) that you wrote in Step 4. Be your answer makes sense. FOR EXAMPLE: If you are trying to find the distance someone travels at 60 miles per hour for 3 hours, be suspicious of your answer if you calculated 18 miles.

7. The final step is to check your answer in the story problem. Remember to first check your answer in the story problem, not in the mathematics statement (or equation) used to solve the story problem. Then, check for careless errors in the mathematics statement (or equation) after you have solved it.

By following these seven steps, you will find story problems are much easier. Many algebra students have difficulty with Step 4 (writing an equation that can used to solve the story problem). The difficulty comes from incorrectly changing words into algebraic symbols or expressions. Please read and study Figures 14 and 15 carefully.

ENGLISH TERM	MATH OPERATION	ENGLISH TERM	MATH OPERATION
Sum Addition Plus More than Increased In excess Greater	+	Per Divide Quotient	÷
		Quantity	( )
Decreased by Less than Subtract Difference Diminished Reduce Take Away	-	Is Was Equal Will be Results	=
		Greater than	>
		Greater than or equal to	≥
Times Percent of Product of	X	Less than	<
		Less than or equal to	≤

Figure 14
Translating English Terms
into Algebraic Symbols

ENGLISH WORDS	EXPRESSION
Ten more than X	X + 10
A number added to 5	5 + X
A number increased by 13	X + 13
5 less than 10	10 - 5
A number decreased by 7	X - 7
Difference between X and 3	X - 3
Difference between 3 an X	3 - X
Twice a number	2X
Ten percent of X	.10X
Ten times X	10X
Quotient of X and 3	X/3
Quotient of 3 and X	3/X
Five is three more than a number	5 = X + 3
The product of two times a number is 10	2X = 10
One half a number is 10	X/2 = 10
Five times the sum of X and 2	5(X + 2)
Seven is greater than X	7 > X
Five times the difference of a number and 4	5(X - 4)
Ten subtracted from 10 times a number is that number plus 5	10X - 10 = X + 5
The sum of 5X and 10 is equal to the product of X and 15	5X + 10 = 15X
The sum of two consecutive integers	(X) + (X + 1)
The sum of two consecutive even integers	(X) + (X + 2)
The sum of two consecutive odd integers	(X) + (X + 2)

Figure 15
Translating English Words
into Algebraic Expressions

SUMMARY

Reading a math textbook is different from reading textbooks on other courses. The chapter lists some steps to help you learn to read your math textbook.

Follow the suggestions on how to do your homework, from the first step of reviewing the textbook (including the examples and lecture notes) to making up note cards.

Solving story problems is a skill and can be learned. The chapter lists seven steps to help you learn how to solve story problems.

Lists have been included to help students with story problems.

HOMEWORK EXERCISES

1. Should you read your math textbook the same way you read your book in English class? If not so, why?

2. Is it true that reading your mathematics textbook takes more time and concentration than your other textbooks? If so, why?

3. a) What are the ten steps to follow when reading a mathematics textbook?
   b) Write at least one or two sentences that wil explain each step.

4. There are eight steps listed in this chapter to help you understand the material in the textbook. Write these eight steps.

5. What should be learned 100 percent before taking a test?

6. What are the two types of goals you can set up before starting your homework? Describe each one.

7. What are the reasons for always finishing your homework by doing a problem correctly?

8. What two things should you do before starting your homework that will improve your homework success?

9. What are some of the benefits of doing your homework neatly?

10. Why should you write down every step of a problem when doing your homework?

11. What happens on math tests when you only memorize how to do the math homework?

12. "Academic suicide" is getting behind in your math homework. Can you explain why?

13. Solving story problems is difficult for most students. Can the skill of solving story problems be learned?

14. All story problems have two main parts. Name them.

15. a) List the seven steps used to solve story problems in an organized manner.
    b) Write two or more sentences about each step to show your understanding of the steps.

16. (For algebra students) Study Figures 14 and 15. What can you add to either list?

17. How can note cards be used to improve math scores? Give an example that is not in the book.

18. Name several advantages of having a study buddy.

19. What should you do after finishing your math homework?

20. Read and study Reference B. List the ten steps to follow when doing your homework.

Notes:

CHAPTER 8
Finding a Good Place to Study

8

Finding a good place to study can improve the quality of work done outside of class. This may not sound important. But it can make a big difference in what you actually learn. It may even reduce the amount of time you will need to study. Wouldn't it be nice to finish your homework one hour sooner than expected?

In choosing a place to study at home, pick one place, one chair, one desk or table as your study area. If you use the kitchen table, pick one chair — preferably one which you do not use during dinner. Now call this chair, "My study chair."

If you have time to study at school, try to study in the same place as much as possible. If you have study hall, pick a seat in the front one-third of "The Golden Triangle of Success." If you arrive at school early or stay late to study (or wait for a ride home), choose the same spot to study. For example, use the same chair at the same table in the library.

Another aspect of choosing the right place to study involves the degree of quiet you need for studying. For some students, a totally quiet room is necessary. Most students, however, can study with a little noise, especially if it is a constant sound like a soft radio station (not loud rock). In fact, the constant sound of soft music or a fan can drown out other noises that may be more distracting. However, do not turn on the television or a loud radio station to drown out other noises. That won't work! Be careful when choosing your study place.

Your study area should be surrounded by signs that tell you to study. One sign should be your study schedule. Attach your study schedule to the inside cover of your notebook and place a copy in your study place at home. Place your study goals and the rewards for getting those goals where they can be seen easily. Do not put up pictures of your girlfriend, boyfriend, your favorite sports car, or trophies in your study area. These could be distracting. Put up pictures indicating your goals after graduation. If you want to attend a specific college, get a certain job, become a nurse, doctor, lawyer, or businessman, post a picture that reminds you of this important goal.

When sitting down to study, the "tools of your trade" are needed. These include paper, pencils, erasers, notebook, textbook, calculator, straight-edge, etc. Anything you might need

"CHOOSING A TIME AND PLACE TO STUDY"

should be within reach. In this way, when you need something you can reach for it, instead of getting up all the time. The problem with getting up is not just the time it takes to get the item, but the time it takes to *warm up* again. After going to get your notes, for example, or to sharpen a pencil, it takes four to five extra minutes to actually continue your studying.

Choosing What to Study First

When planning your study time arrange subjects in order of their difficulty. In other words, start with your most difficult subject — usually math — and work towards your easiest course. If you study math first, you will be more alert and motivated. Don't wait to study math until after you have studied your other subjects. You will probably tire easily, become confused, and quit. Your easier courses may also be more interesting to you. You are less likely to quit when you are getting tired if the subject is easy and interests you. REMEMBER: *Study math first.*

When and How to Study

Deciding when to study different types of material is part of having good study habits. In general, the best time to study math is as soon as possible after the mathematics class.

Most forgetting occurs right after learning the material. In other words, you are going to forget most of what you have learned in the first hours after class. To stop this from happening, you need to recall or review the class material. The easiest way to do this is to re-work your notes as soon as possible after class. Do this even before you sit down to actually do your homework, if possible. Reviewing your notes will help you recall the information and make it easier to understand your homework assignment.

Now cover up your note page so that you can only see the left column (See Figures 12 and 13). Look at the key words and ideas and recall these meanings. Mark the key words and ideas you could not remember for future study.

Learning new material should be done during the first part of the study period. If your homework assignment is to complete the chapter exercises, organize your study time as follows:

First, read the textbook section and review your notes as explained in Chapter VII. Try the sample problems on your own, then check your answers against those in the textbook. Then try a few of the odd numbered problems in your homework assignment. The answers to the odd numbered problems are usually found in the back of the textbook. You can then check your answers against the textbook. If your answers are the same as those printed in the back of the text, complete all of the chapter exercises. If your answers are not correct, re-read both your textbook and your notes and try again. Once your homework assignment is completed, the last part of your study period can be used to review for an upcoming test. You can also read ahead and preview the next chapter.

It is important to complete your chapter exercises the day the homework is given. Do not try to learn new material the night before a test or exam. You will be setting yourself up for test anxiety and maybe failing the test.

Remember, learning new material should be done as soon after class as possible and during the first part of the study period. If you are tired and try to learn new material, it becomes more difficult to remember. It takes more effort to learn new material when you are tired than it does to review old material.

The best time to review old material for a test or exam, however, may be right before going to sleep. There is less brain activity and less physical distractions between the time you review the material and the time of the test. Get a good nights sleep before taking the test to allow your memory to recall the information necessary to answer the questions.

Importance of Study Breaks

Psychologists have discovered that learning decreases if you study for long periods of time without study breaks. For most students, twenty-five to forty-five minutes is the best length of time to study before taking a short break. If you study for only twenty minutes and feel your mind wandering, take a five or ten minute break. Then return to your studying. If you continue to force yourself to study without a break, you will not learn the material.

If you still can not study after taking a break, think about your reasons for studying. Think about what is required to graduate. It will probably relate to the fact that you will have to pass math. Think about how studying math today will help you pass the next test. This will increase your chances of passing the course and graduating.

At this point, on an index card write down three positive statements about yourself and three positive statements about studying. Look at this index card every time you have a study problem.

SUMMARY

Choosing a good study area at home and at school with the least amount of distractions can increase you learning potential.

Be prepared with your "tools of the trade". Organize your study time by studying math first (new material, then review). Take a study break after twenty-five to forty-five minutes of studying. These techniques can improve learning skills and lead to higher grades.

For additional information read Reference C (Ten Steps to Improving Your Study Skills) and Reference D (Suggestions to Teachers for Improving Student Math Study Skills).

HOMEWORK EXERCISES

1. How can the quality of work done outside of class be improved?

2. Why is soft music or the constant sound of a fan desirable for some students when doing homework?

3. Why should you turn the television off when doing your homework?

4. What types of signs or pictures should be posted in your study area?

5. What items would be distracting in your study area?

6. What are the "tools of your trade" as they apply to math homework?

7. Why is it important to have the "tools of your trade" within reach?

8. In what order do you need to study your courses?

9. What are some reasons for studying math first?

10. The best time to study math is as soon as possible after math class. Why?

11. What should you do with your notes before actually starting your home work?

12. When should you learn new material?

13. When the written part of your homework is finished, what should you do with the remaining time in your study period?

14. Studying new material the night before a test is dangerous. Why?

15. When is a good time to review old material for a test? Why?

16. How long can most students study before needing a break?

17. If you force yourself to study without a break, what can happen?

18. What should you do if you can not start studying, even after taking a break?

19. Read, study and copy on your own paper, Reference C - Ten Steps to Improving Your Study Skills.

20. Read and study Reference D.

Notes:

CHAPTER 9
Memory: The Long and the Short of It

9

Learning is the process of gaining knowledge and understanding a subject or skill. It is the process of really knowing a subject. Learning involves studying, listening, reading, watching, and doing. Researchers have found that there are only three ways we really learn. They are:

* conditioning
* thinking
* combination of conditioning and thinking

Learning by Conditioning and Thinking

Conditioning is learning things by repeating or by doing the same thing over and over again. Conditioning takes little or no thinking. Conditioned learning uses rote memory. This means you repeat or do something over and over again, though you do not understand why you are doing it. It is learning by routine or repetition carried out without understanding. It could be considered mechanical. FOR EXAMPLE: Learning the ABC's as a child by repeating after your mother, father, brother or sister. Or learning to type by practicing on a typewriter.

Thinking, on the other hand, is learning by observing, processing, and understanding the material. It is the action of using one's mind to produce thoughts. It involves forming mental pictures and clear ideas.

The most successful way to learn math is not by conditioning or thinking alone. It is by a combination of thinking and conditioning. The best learning combination is to learn by thinking first and conditioning second.

Memory - Processing and Storing Information

Memory is different from learning. Memory is the process of getting information through your senses and storing the information in your mind. Recalling information for later use completes the process. You get information through your *sensory input* by seeing, hearing, feeling, and touching. Sensory input is the first stage of memory. The sensory register is the second stage of memory. It holds an image of each sensory experience for a short time, only until it can be used. Once the information is used, it is stored in short-term memory. If the information is not used immediately, it is forgotten. The sensory registry helps us go from one situation to the next without cluttering up our minds.

Short-Term Memory

Short-term memory is the third stage of memory which allows you to remember facts for quick use. These facts are soon forgotten. Examples of short-term memory are:
* Looking up a number in the telephone directory and remembering it long
    enough to dial, then forgetting it immediately
* Learning the name of a person at a large party or in a class but forgetting it
    completely within a few minutes
* Cramming for a test and forgetting most of the material before taking the test

Remembering for a short time is not hard to do. By making an effort, you can remember a math fact or formula from the sensory register. Then, you can put it into short- term memory.

You heard your teacher explain the process of adding fractions and you read it in your textbook. You recognize it and register it in your mind as something to remember for a short time.

FOR EXAMPLE: When you are studying fractions you tell yourself that you need a common denominator to add fractions. By telling yourself to remember that fact, you can remember it because you have put it in short-term memory. Short-term memory is the part of your memory where information can be remembered for only a short period of time.

An important fact to remember, though, is that the amount of information you can keep in short-term memory is small. You may be able to tell yourself to remember one phone number or a few formulas but not a dozen numbers or formulas. To remember more facts or ideas, especially at test time, a better system than short-term memory is required.

Researchers have found that short-term memory can not store a large amount of information. Also, items placed into short-term memory usually fade fast. An example is the telephone number you learned just long enough to dial. Short-term memory is useful in helping you concentrate on a few things at a time. It is not the best way to learn mathematics. A major problem is when students use short-term memory to do their homework. They think they know how to do the math problem. But they have only remembered how to do the steps long enough to do the homework; then forgetting occurs.

Long-Term Memory

Long-term memory is the fourth stage of memory which keeps unlimited information for long periods of time. It is considered to be a person's total knowledge.

Long-term memory is not just remembering more and more unrelated facts or ideas. Basically, long-term memory is organizing your short-term memories into meaningful information. It involves thinking them out, understanding their meaning, and mentally going over them. Without going over the information, thinking about it often or writing it on paper, the information will not be put into long-term memory.

The main problem students face is getting learned material from short-term memory into long-term memory. Putting mathematics information into long-term memory is not done by just doing your homework. You need to develop good thinking habits to place important material into long-term memory.

The last step in the memory process is recalling the information for actual use. Recalling information from memory is most important during tests. This process can be blocked by having trouble putting short-term memory into long-term memory. Test anxiety and poor test taking skills are other blocks to recalling information.

Understanding the stages of memory will help you answer this common question about mathematics: "How can I understand the steps to solve a math problem one day and forget how to solve a similar problem two days later?"

There are two good answers to the question. After learning how to solve the problem, the

"CONVERTING MATERIAL FROM SHORT-TERM
TO LONG-TERM MEMORY"

process or steps were not practiced enough. A second answer is that you did get it into long-term memory but the information was not reviewed enough to keep it there. Either answer tells what happens if students do not rehearse or review their new math material enough. See Figure 16 for a better understanding of the Stages of Memory.

Putting Information from Short-Term
to Long-Term Memory

There are several ways to help put information from short-term to long-term memory. These include developing a positive study attitude, decreasing distractions, organizing material, reciting facts, using mental pictures, using association and memory devices, and many others. (See Reference E.)

Having a positive attitude about studying will help you concentrate and will improve your memory. This does not mean you have to like studying math. But you at least need a positive attitude about learning the information.

Look at studying as an opportunity to learn rather than an unpleasant task. Tell yourself you can learn the material. Learning the material will help you pass the exam, pass the course, improve your grades, graduate, get accepted to college, etc.

Use the "Full mind concept" to decrease distractions. Imagine that your mind is completely filled with thoughts of learning math. Then, other distracting thoughts can not enter. Your mind has only one way which opens it to thoughts about mathematics when you are doing your math homework or studying math.

Improve your study concentration by counting the number of distractions for each study session. Place a sheet of paper by your book. When you catch yourself not concentrating, put the letter "C" on the sheet of paper. This will remind you to concentrate and get back to work. Count up the number of "C's" after each study period and watch the number decrease.

Organizing the material will help you learn. Learn and memorize ideas and facts in groups. Put the material to be learned into categories. Do not learn isolated facts.

Reciting facts is one of the best ways to get information into long-term memory. Say facts and ideas out loud. This improves your ability to think and remember. If you are in study hall and can not recite out loud, recite the material to yourself. As you are reciting, emphasize the important words.

Writing and reciting the material at the same time is even a better way to learn. After you

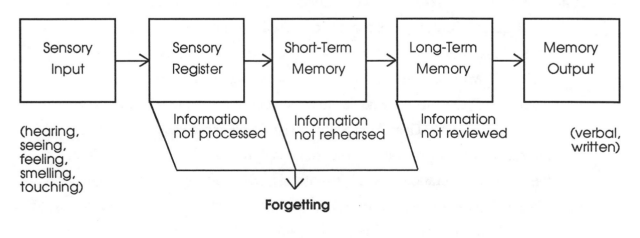

Figure 16
Stages of Memory

correctly recite the material back to yourself one time, do not stop. Do it five or ten more times to over learn it.

Use mental pictures or diagrams to help you learn the material. Mental pictures and diagrams involve 100 percent of your brain power. Picture the steps to solve difficult math problems in your mind.

Use association learning to help you remember better. Make a connection or relationship between new information to be learned and old information you already know. The recalling of old facts will help you remember new facts.

> EXAMPLE 1: When studying a lesson on fractions you learn that a fraction is made up of a numerator and a denominator. How will you remember which is which? One way to remember that the bottom number is the denominator is that the first letter of the word denominator is "D" which could stand for "DOWN". Therefore, you remember that the denominator is always "down" or the bottom number.

> EXAMPLE 2: When learning the distributive law of multiplication over addition, such as a(b+c), remember that distribution is giving out a product. Just remember the distributor is "a" and is giving its products to "b" and "c".

Make up your own association to remember math properties and laws. REMEMBER: the more personal the association, the more likely you will remember it.

The use of memory devices is another way to help you remember. Use easily remembered words, phrases or rhymes associated with difficult to remember principles or facts.

> EXAMPLE 1: Many students become confused when using the Order of Operations. These students mix up the order of the steps in solving a problem. FOR EXAMPLE, Dividing instead of first adding the numbers in the parenthesis. One memory device to remember the Order of Operation is "Please Excuse My Dear Aunt Sally". The first letter in each of the words represents the math operation to be completed from the first to the last. Thus, the Order of Operations are (P) Parenthesis, (E) Exponents, (M) Multiplication, (D) Division, (A) Addition, and (S) Subtraction.

> EXAMPLE 2: FOIL is one of the most common math memory devices used by algebra students. FOIL is used to remember the procedure to multiply two

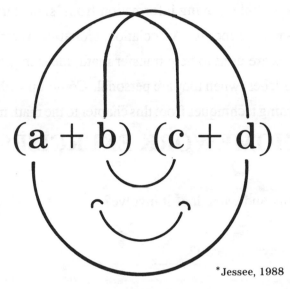

F (a) (c)
O (a) (d)
I (b) (c)
L (b) (d)

$$(a + b) \ (c + d)$$

*Jessee, 1988

Figure 17
The FOIL Method

binomials. The letters in the word FOIL stand for First, Outside, Inside, and Last. To get the first part of your answer, multiply the first parts of the binomials. Next, add the outside product to the inside product to get the middle part of your answer. Lastly, multiply the last parts of the binomials to get the last part of your answer. Another way to remember FOIL is to look at the face in Figure 17.

Use your imagination to make up your own memory devices to remember mathematical rules. Remember to review Reference E for even more ideas.

SUMMARY

The most successful way to learn math is a combination of thinking and conditioning. Conditioning is learning by repeating. Thinking is learning by using your mind to produce thoughts.

Learning memory techniques is based on understanding how receiving, storing and recalling information relate to each other.

Many students have trouble moving information from short-term memory to long-term memory. This is an important process. Association, recitation, forming mental pictures and the use of memory devices are used to help transfer math ideas into long-term memory.

Memory devices work best when they are personal. Come up with your own list. Use your imagination to adopt learning techniques from this chapter to the math material you are learning.

HOMEWORK EXERCISES

1. What is learning and what does it involve?

2. List the three ways we learn?

3. a) What does learning by conditioning mean?
   b) Give an example of conditioned learning.

4. How do the authors define thinking?

5. What does thinking involve?

6. The most successful way to learn math is by a combination of thinking and conditioning. Which should come first?

7. How do the authors define memory?

8. What is your sensory register?

9. How do you receive information through your sensory register?

10. Why do you have to process information from your sensory register, where it is stored?

11. Once information is processed from your sensory register, where is it stored?

12. a) What is the third stage of memory called?
    b) What is the purpose of this stage?

13. Give at least three examples of short-term memory.

14. Can you store a large amount of information in your short-term memory?

15. If using short-term memory is not the best way to learn mathematics, why is it useful?

16. a) What is the fourth stage of memory called?
    b) What is the purpose of this stage?

17. What is considered to be a persons total knowledge?

18. How is information processed into long-term memory?

19. One of the main problems students have in learning mathematics is converting material from short-term memory into long-term memory. What do you need to develop to do this?

20. Name three things that block your ability to recall information.

21. Students sometimes say they understand the steps to solve a problem today but forget the steps two days later. What two things would explain this?

22. What are some ways used to help convert information from short-term memory to long-term memory?

23. How can a positive attitude about studying mathematics help you?

24. What is the "full mind concept"?

25. What is one way to decrease the number of distractions when you are studying?

26. Organizing material will help you learn. How would you do this?

27. What is one of the best ways to get information into long-term memory?

28. Do mental pictures or diagrams help you to learn material?

29. a) What does association learning mean?
    b) Give an example of learning by association. Can you think of any others?

30. a) What are memory devices?
    b) Give an example of a memory device.

31. Read and study Reference E.

CHAPTER 10
Tests: How to Show What You Know

10

Test grades are important to you. At the end of the semester or year, your teacher will average your test results. This will determine your final letter grade. Read this chapter carefully to learn how to improve your test grades.

Comparing Homework Problems to the Actual Test

Many students believe that doing all their homework ensures an "A" or "B" on tests. This is far from true. Doing all the homework and getting the right answers is very different in many ways from taking tests.

1) There is little anxiety while doing your homework. A test situation is just the opposite. *Anxiety may be very high during a test.*

2) You can take your time while doing homework. A test situation is quite different. You may have to finish the test in thirty, forty-five or fifty-five minutes.

3) If you get stuck on a homework problem, your textbook and notes are there to refer to. During a test you have no book or notes to help you. You must depend upon your memory and understanding.

4) Once you learn to do several problems in a homework assignment, the rest are similar. In a test the problems may be different types and all mixed up.

5) Textbooks have the answers to the odd-numbered problems. This means you already have the answers to over half of your homework problems.

Doing your assigned homework every school day is very important. But do not develop a false hope by believing you can make an "A" or "B" by **just** doing your homework.

Making Your Own Practice Tests

Making your own practice tests is the best way to determine if you are ready for an important test. You can write your practice test by choosing problems from the chapter sections and chapter review. Choose problems from the examples in this book to prepare a practice test. Do not stop there.

Go to the homework problems from each section, and finally to the chapter review exercise and pick more problems. Do not choose the easiest problems or the hardest problems.

Most teachers pick problems of average degree of difficulty for their tests. Once you have the problems for the practice test, wait a day. Then, take the test using the same amount of time your teacher allows.

Problems chosen from the textbook examples or from odd- numbered homework problems can be checked from the book. If not, get with your study buddy or teacher to check your practice test.

REMEMBER: Practice tests are the best way to find your problem areas. However, to be effective they must be written three days before the real test. You must allow time to get help for the problems that you missed.

NOTE: Tests are not mysterious. They do not come from the sky. Your teacher makes the "real test" just as suggested above. Chances are, you have actually chosen some of the same problems (with different numbers maybe) that will be on the test. That gives you an advantage. As you make up more practice tests, the questions will become more similar to the real test.

Holding a Group Study Session

Holding a group study session is another way to prepare for an important test by taking practice tests. Hold the group study session several days before the test.

Each student should prepare a test with ten questions. On the back of the test the answers should be worked out step-by-step. When your study group gets together, each member of the group gives his/her test to all the group members. Once the tests have been completed, answers are checked and problems discussed by the group.

The group study session method of taking practice tests can actually be a fun way to prepare for a math test. You can increase your testing skills, find problems areas, and help your classmates do the same. Just make sure your group study sessions do not turn into a party.

General Pre-Test Principles

These general principles are important when taking any kind of test. Please remember to follow them.

1) *Get a good night's sleep before taking a test.* This is true for any test, but especially for important math tests. You can't study all night and perform well on your test with three or four hours of sleep. You will do better to get seven or eight hours of sleep. This way you will be fresh enough to use your memory to recall information needed to answer the questions.

2) *Start studying for the test at least three days ahead of time.*

3) *Review only already learned material the night before or the day of the test.*

Ten Steps to Better Test Taking

Once you begin a test, follow the ten steps to better test taking listed below:

Step 1: *As soon as you receive your test, write down the information you think you might forget.* Before doing *anything,* first write down formulas, proper ties or figures you might not remember. This is called the *first memory facts list.* The facts list may contain important information you will need to answer the test questions. FOR EXAMPLE: Suppose you have been studying motion problems in class. You think you will need the formula- Distance equals Rate times Time. On your first facts list you write on your test paper, D = R X T. Then, when you get to a motion problem, you refer to the facts list rather than having to recall the formula at that time.

Step 2: *Preview the test.* Now put your name on the test, then look over the entire test to see what it is like. Look for the type of problems and how many points each question is worth. Put marks by the easy problems as you preview.

Step 3: *Do a second facts list.* For the second facts list write down any information you think of while previewing the test. As you looked over the questions, you might have thought of a fact or formula that will be needed to answer a specific question. Write it down now.

Step 4: *Set up a test schedule.* Decide the best way to get the most points in the least amount of time. This is usually done by answering the easiest problems first. Do not forget about the easy problems you already marked. In most math tests, the easier problems are near the beginning of the first page; you need to answer them correctly and quickly. This will give you more time for harder problems.

You might have some test questions that are worth more points than other test questions. In some tests, word problems are worth five points and other problems worth two or three points. This might mean working the problems worth two or three points first and leaving the more difficult word problems for last. If you have a fifty minute test then more than half the problems should be done in twenty-five minutes.

Step 5: *Answer the easiest problems first and review the answers to see if they make sense.* Do the already marked easy questions first. Answers should be reasonable. FOR EXAMPLE: The answer to a land motion problem can not be 1000 miles per hour. Clearly write down each step of the problem you are working in order to at least get partial credit if your answer is wrong. Most math teachers give partial credit. Teachers who see that the student knows how to solve the problem but makes a careless mistake can get points. Isn't a point or two better than none?

Step 6: *If you find a problem that you do not know how to do, skip it.* This could be a type of problem you have never seen before or a problem where you get stuck on the second or third step. In both cases, skip the problem and go on to the next. Do not waste time here if there are other problems you can solve.

Step 7: *Review the skipped questions.* Return to the skipped problems. Think of how you have solved other similar problems. Try to remember how the instructor solved this type of problem on the board.

Step 8: *Guess at the remaining problems or do as much work on them as you can.* Try to get something down on paper. Even if your answer is wrong, there may be something in your work that deserves partial credit. However, do not waste too much time on guessing or trying to work problems you know nothing about. At least re-write the problem. This may help you remember the next step. If you put nothing down, you will get zero points for the problem.

Step 9: *Review the test for careless mistakes.* Students usually lose two to five points on careless mistakes. This could mean the difference between receiving an "A" or "B" or a "D" or "F". Do not forget to review.

Step 10: *Use all the allowed test time.* Review each problem. Check your answers by substituting the answers back into the problem or by doing the opposite function required to answer the questions. If you can not check the problems in either of these ways, rework the problems on a separate sheet of paper. Then, compare the answers. For answers that do not match, compare both sets of work to find your mistake. Do not leave the test room unless you have reviewed each problem three times or until the bell rings. REMEMBER: *There is no prize for handing your test in first.* If your teacher allows you to turn in your scratch paper, staple it to the math test. Handing it in can have several advantages:

    A. If you miscopied the answer from the scratch paper, you will probably get credit for the answer.

    B. If you get an answer wrong due to a careless mistake, your work on the scratch paper could give you a few points.

    C. If you get the problem wrong, it will be easier to find the mistakes when the instructor reviews the test. This may prevent you from making the same mistakes on the next math test.

If you are not sure about handing in your scratch paper, check with your math teacher. If it is allowed, it may get you extra points or improve your next test grade.

Six Types of Test-Taking Errors

To do better on tests in the future, look at some of the tests you have taken in the past. Look for the following kinds of errors:

(1) misread direction errors

(2) careless errors

(3) fundamental errors

(4) application errors

(5) examination errors

(6) study errors

"SIX TYPES OF TEST-TAKING ERRORS"

Misread direction errors occur when you do not read the directions or you do not understand the directions.

EXAMPLE 1: In arithmetic you have this problem to solve: John traveled 60 miles the first day, 30 miles the second day, and 60 miles the third day. Find the average number of miles John traveled per day. Some students add 60 + 30 + 60 = 150 and leave 150 for their answer. They did not read the question through to see that they need the average number of miles traveled per day, not the total number of miles traveled.

EXAMPLE 2: In algebra you have this type of problem to solve: $(X + 1) (X + 1)$ Some students will try to solve for X, but the problem only calls for multiplication. You would solve for X only if you have an equation such as $(X + 1) (X + 1) = 0$.

EXAMPLE 3: Another common mistake is not reading the directions before doing several word problems. All too often, when the test is returned, you find only three out of the five problems had to be completed. Even if you did get all five correct, it cost you valuable time which could have been used on other problems.

To avoid misread direction errors, read all the directions. If you do not understand them, ask your teacher to explain them.

Careless errors are mistakes made which you should catch easily as you review the test. Good and poor math students make careless errors. These errors can easily cost a student the difference of a letter grade on a test. In algebra, a careless error in math tests is dropping the sign. EXAMPLE: $-3X(2X) = 6X^2$, instead of $-6X^2$ which is the correct answer.

Another careless error is not simplifying your answer. EXAMPLE: Leaving 5/15 as your answer, instead of simplifying it to 1/3.

When working with students who make careless errors, these questions are asked.

1. "How many points did you lose due to careless errors?"
2. "How much time was left in the class period when you handed in your test?"

Students who lose test points to careless errors are giving away points. They do this by handing in their papers before the test period ends.

To reduce careless errors you must know the type of careless errors you make. You also need to recognize them when reviewing your test. FOR EXAMPLE: Your most common careless error is not simplifying the answer. Then, you must review each answer as if it were a new problem, and try to simplify it.

Fundamental errors are mistakes made when you do not understand the properties or principles needed to work the problem. Fundamental errors, if not corrected, will follow you from test to test causing loss of points each time. Some common fundamental errors are not knowing:

$$\frac{1}{3} + \frac{2}{5} = \frac{11}{15} \text{, not } \frac{3}{8}$$

$$3 < 5 \text{ but } -3 > -5$$

$$\frac{5}{0} \text{ is undefined, not } 0$$

$$(A + X)/X \text{ is not simplified to } A$$

$$3 + 2 \times 5 = 13 \text{ not } 25$$

Fundamental errors must be corrected to improve your next math test score.

Students who have a number of fundamental errors will fail the next test and the course. Why? Because the math properties and principles are not understood.

Going back to rework the incorrectly answered problems is not good enough. You must go back to your textbook and notes to learn why you missed those types of problems. It is not enough to just do one type of problem. You must learn to work those types of problems in the future by setting up pages in the back of your notebook for these fundamental errors. These pages should relate to each test.

Label the first page of your notebook Chapter 1 — just as it appears in your text book. Then, write down the fundamental problems you missed and the correct way to do them. Then, do five more similar problems. Write in your own words how to do the problems and the page number where you learned the correct information. Get help from your instructor now, if you can not figure out how to do the problem.

Application errors occur when you know the fundamental principle, but you can not apply it to the problem. Application errors are usually found in word problems. Even some better math students become frustrated with application errors. They understand the material but can not apply it to the problem.

To reduce application errors, try to predict the type of application or word problem that will be on the test. Then think through and practice solving those types of problems using the fundamental principles you know.

> EXAMPLE: Your father drove at an average rate of 60 or 2 hours. Find the total distance traveled. You certainly know how to multiply 60 X 2 = 120. But in a word problem you may not know exactly what math operation to use. You would then go back to your textbook and notes to review and practice time, rate and distance problems.

Application errors are common with word problems. When doing word problems, look for key phrases. Always re-read the question to make sure you have applied the right math operation to answer it. Application errors can be avoided with enough practice and insight.

Examination errors apply to the specific way you take tests. Some students make the same types of examination errors over and over again. Look at your old math tests to find out if you have made any of the stated examination errors. If you did, replace them with good test taking habits. The result will be higher test scores. The following are examination errors that can cause you to lose points on a test.

1. *Missing more questions in the first third or last third of a test is considered an examination error.* Missing more questions in the first third of a test could bc causcd by carelessness when doing easy problems. Another reason is that you are experiencing test anxiety. Missing questions in the last third could be due to the difficulty of the last questions. It also may be due to your desire to finish the test quickly. FOR EXAMPLE: You consistently miss more ques tions in a certain part of the test. Use your remaining test time to review that section of the test first.

2. *Not completing a problem to its last step is another examination error.* If you have this bad habit, review the last step of every test problem first. Then, review the whole problem from step one.

3. *Changing test answers from correct ones to incorrect ones is a problem for some students.* Review your old math tests. Find out if you are a good or bad answer changer. If you seem to be a bad answer changer, only change

answers if you can prove to yourself that the changed answer is correct.

4. *Getting stuck on one problem and spending too much time on it is another examination error.* You need to set a time limit first on each problem before moving to the next problem. Working too long on a single problem without success will increase test anxiety and waste valuable time. This time could be used in solving other problems or in reviewing your test.

5. *Rushing through the easiest part of the test and making careless mistakes is a common examination error for the better math student.* Some students have the bad   habit of getting more points taken off for the easy problems than for the hard problems. If this is you, then review the easy problems first and review the hard problems last.

6. *Miscopying an answer from your scratch work to the test paper is an examination error.* It is important to write down each step on your test to allow for partial credit. However, if you do use scratch paper, be careful to compare your last problem step with the answer on the test paper. In addition, hand in your scratch paper with the test.

7. *Leaving answers blank is an examination error.* Leaving answers blank will get you zero points. If you look at a problem and can not figure out how to solve it, do not leave it blank. Write down some information about the problem or try at least to do the first step. REMEMBER: Writing down the first step of a problem is the key to solving the problem and obtaining partial credit. In other words, re-write the problem so it looks like you tried to work it.

8. *The last major examination error is not following the ten steps to better test taking.* Think about your test taking procedures. Try to follow the ten steps to better test taking. Try to correct the eight common test taking errors. The result will be higher test scores!

Study errors are the last type of mistakes to look for in reviewing your past math tests. Study error occurs when you study the wrong type of material or do not spend enough time on important material. Try to find out if you missed problems because you did not practice that type of problem enough. Another study error is that you did not practice the problem. Study errors may take some time to track down, but correcting them will help on future tests.

Objective and Essay Test Questions

Sometimes mathematics tests have objective test questions. Objective test questions are in the form of true and false, multiple choice and matching. To better understand the procedures in taking an objective test, read Reference F - <u>Taking an Objective Test</u>.

Very few mathematics tests have essay questions. However, improving the skills required to take an essay test could give you more time for studying mathematics. Read Reference G - <u>Answering an Essay Test</u>.

SUMMARY

Test grades are important. They are used to determine a final average for the course. Being successful with your homework does not necessarily mean you will be successful on tests.

Completing a practice test at least three days before an exam can locate areas needing improvement.

Holding a group study session before a test can be helpful unless it turns into a party.

Start studying for a test at least three days in advance and get a good night's sleep just before test day.

Follow the <u>Ten Steps to Better Test Taking</u> to obtain the most amount of points in the least amount of time.

Be aware of the six types of errors students make on tests. Go over previous math tests to locate some of your test taking errors and try to prevent them in the future.

Reference F, <u>Taking an Objective Test</u>, Reference G, <u>Answering an Essay Test</u> and Reference H, <u>Studying for Exams</u> are located in the back of this book.

HOMEWORK EXERCISES

1. Why are test grades important to you?

2. Give at least five reasons why knowing how to do all your homework will not insure an "A" or a "B" on tests.

3. Making up your own practice test is the best way to determine if you are ready for a test. How would you make up a practice test?

4. Explain how a group study session can be used to help you do well on a test.

5. Three general pre-test principles are listed in this book. Write them down now.

6. a) List the 10 steps to better test taking.
   b) Write at least two sentences about each step to show your understanding of the steps.

7. What are the advantages of turning in your scratch paper?

8. a) What are the six types of test taking errors?
   b) Give an example of each type of error. Can you think of any others?

9. Review your last major chapter(s) test and write down how many points you lost for each test-taking error. Give examples.

10. a) List the eight examination errors.
    b) Write at least two sentences about each error to show your understanding.

11. Read and study Reference F - <u>Taking an Objective Test</u>.

12. Read and study Reference G - <u>Answering an Essay Test</u>.

13. Read and study Reference H - <u>Studying for Exams</u>.

Notes:

CHAPTER 11

Now It is Up to You

11

Do you remember the section you studied in Chapter Three on Bloom's research regarding grades? According to Bloom, fifty percent of your grade comes from intelligence and entry level skills. Twenty-five percent of your grade is accounted for by quality of instruction. The final twenty-five percent is determined by your personal characteristics.

You can improve your grade by using all three of the mentioned areas. However, it is the last area, your personal characteristics, where you have the most control. Think about that. Twenty-five percent of your grade is accounted for by something that you have the most control over. That is why this last chapter is titled, **It's Up To You.**

Let's say you want to have a better understanding of mathematics and earn higher grades. Then, concentrate your efforts on improving your personal characteristics.

In addition to your personal characteristics there are three last areas to be discussed. These will enable you to take control over mathematics. The three areas are developing internal control, avoiding learned helplessness, and decreasing procrastination.

Developing Internal Control

Students who feel they have power within themselves to control their own situations have internal control. Internal students believe that they can overcome most situations. Why? Because the results depend on *THEIR* behavior or personal characteristics. Internal students accept the responsibility for their behavior. They realize, for example, that studying today will help pass the mathematics test scheduled for next week. Internal students can delay getting rewards now to getting rewards later. FOR EXAMPLE: They can study for a test now and go to a party later in the week.

External students, on the other hand, feel that conditions beyond their control stop them from getting good grades. These students blame their teachers, school rules, or even home conditions for their poor grades. They feel they can not do anything about their problems because outside forces are in control.

For you to be successful in math you need to have internal control. *YOU NEED TO ACCEPT RESPONSIBILITY FOR YOUR SUCCESS.*

In general, students who are internal will work harder to meet their educational goals than will external students. The internal student can relate today's actions (studying, textbook reading) to getting a college degree and a good job. External students, on the other hand, can not connect the behavior of studying today with getting good grades and good jobs. Thus, internals are more oriented towards making high mathematics grades than externals.

Externals can change into internals. Here's how you can take more responsibility for your life and obtain your education.

You can take more responsibility by developing and accomplishing short-term goals and long-term goals. Short- term goals are goals developed and completed within a day or week. For instance, a goal of studying math today between 7:00 p.m. and 9:00 p.m. is short term. A long term goal, for example, could be earning an "A" or "B" in the math course for the semester or year.

The steps to obtaining your short-term goals or long-term goals must be thought out or written down. Rewarding yourself after meeting short-term goals increases your internal control. This will help you see the connection between studying and getting good grades. Short-term goal successes lead to greater successes in obtaining long-term goals.

Avoiding Learned Helplessness

As students become more external they develop learned helplessness. Learned helplessness means believing that other people or influences from teachers or the system controls what happens to them. These students adopt the attitude, "Why try?" Students who have failed or made low grades in mathematics several times may develop learned helplessness.

Total lack of motivation to finish math assignments is a good example of learned helplessness. Students who develop learned helplessness can break this bad habit. In the past, a student may have finished the math assignments but did not pass the test. This may have happened many times in the past. This led to the attitude, "Why try?" because the student tried several times in the past to be successful in math and still failed the tests.

The problem with this thinking is the *way* the student actually tried to pass the math course. Their learning process, anxiety reduction, and test taking techniques were not as good as the ones discussed in this book. It was like trying to remove a flat tire with a pair of pliers instead of using a tire iron.

Now that you have the *tire iron* (SUCCESSFUL MATH STUDY SKILLS), the question is, "Are you motivated enough to put forth the effort to use the *tire iron* and make a good grade?" Take responsibility for yourself and you are on your way to being successful at math.

Overcoming Procrastination, Fear of Failure and Fear of Success

Procrastination is putting off your studying. This is a bad way to take control over mathematics. Students may procrastinate by not reading the textbook or not doing their homework. This may be due to fear of failure, fear of success, or rebellion against authority. Some students who fear failure, procrastinate to avoid any true measurement of how good they are in math. By waiting too long to begin work on a paper or studying for a test, real ability (smartness) is never measured. Thus, students can never learn the degree (good or bad) of their ability to do math.

Other students who have fear of failure could be perfectionists. Perfectionists want to do everything perfect. Perfectionists usually expect more of themselves than can be possibly obtained.

FOR EXAMPLE: A 9th grade algebra student making a "C" in math decides to set a goal to make an "A" the following year. After making a "C" in the first major test in geometry, the student becomes angry. The student starts to procrastinate and believes the goal of making an "A" is now impossible. Now the students attitude is if I cannot make an "A", why study at all.

Being a perfectionist is not related to how high you set the goal but the unrealistic nature of the goal itself.

Fear of success means not putting an all-out effort towards becoming successful. Some students believe becoming too successful will lose them friends. Guilt from becoming more successful than family or close friends is also a problem.

"REBELLING AGAINST AUTHORITY"

This *fear of success* can be generalized as *fear of competition* in making good grades. These students do not fear the chance of making low grades when competing. They fear they will not be liked by others, if they make high grades.

FOR EXAMPLE: A math student may fear that by studying too much she will make the highest test grade. She has more fear that students will not like her due to her high grades than the fear of just making average grades. These students need to take pride in their learning ability. Let the other students take responsibility for their own grades.

Rebelling Against Authority

The third cause of procrastination is the desire to rebel against authority. Students believe that by handing in their homework late or by missing the test they can get back at the teacher.

These students usually lack self-esteem. They would rather blame the teacher for their poor grades than take responsibility for completing their homework. Rebelling against the teacher gives them a false sense of control over their lives. However, the rebelling students do the exact thing expected of them by their teachers: make poor grades. These students discover, often too late, they are only hurting themselves.

Procrastination is not a simple issue. Students procrastinate for various reasons. Procrastination, though, mainly protects self-esteem. Most students who procrastinate have poor mathematics grades.

SUMMARY

Improving your personal characteristics will increase your understanding of mathematics and earn you a higher grade. Of the three areas that account for your grade, you have the most control over your personal characteristics.

Successful students have internal control, avoid learned helplessness, and decrease procrastination.

You can start becoming internal by taking the responsibility for following the suggestions in Chapters Six through Ten. You should set up and accomplish realistic short-term goals. You can avoid learned helplessness by not giving up on making a good grade in mathematics. You can start decreasing procrastination by following the suggestions in Chapter Four (<u>Budgeting Your Time</u>) and Chapter Five (<u>Math Anxiety and How to Reduce It</u>). Also, remember not to use procrastination as a reason for doing poorly in mathematics.

NOTE: Students who have followed the suggestions in this book have improved their mathematics grades when compared to other students who did not use these suggestions.

HOMEWORK EXERCISES

1. What accounts for 25 percent of your math grade that you have the most control over?

2. What should be the results of you improving your personal characteristics?

3. What are three areas that will enable you to take control of mathematics?

4. In your own words, describe an internal student.

5. In your own words, describe an external student.

6. Does an internal or an external student accept responsibility for his/her behavior?

7. Who or what do external students blame for poor grades?

8. To be successful in mathematics you need to have internal control. (True or False)

9. Is it possible for external students to change into internal students? If so, how?

10. What are short-term goals? Give an example.

11. Give an example of a long-term goal.

12. What does <u>learned helplessness</u> mean?

13. Give an example of learned helplessness.

14. a) Is it possible to break the habit of learned helplessness?
    b) How would you break the habit of learned helplessness?

15. Write in your own words what procrastinate means as it
    applies to math.

16. Why do some math students procrastinate?

17. What is <u>fear of failure</u>? Give an example.

18. What does <u>fear of success</u> mean?

19. What are the results of fear of success?

20. A cause of procrastination is to rebel against authority.
    a) Give an example of this kind of procrastination.
    b) Who is really being hurt when using this kind of procrastination?

21. Schedule an appointment to meet with your math teacher at least once during
    the fall and once during the spring to talk about your progress.

GLOSSARY

GLOSSARY

ACRONYM — a memory device in which one or more words are made up of the first letter of each of the words comprising the information you wish to remember. For example, ROY G BIV is an acronym representing the colors of the rainbow — red, orange, yellow, green, blue, indigo and violet.

ASSOCIATION LEARNING — a memory technique used to relate new information to be learned to old information you already know.

CONDITIONED RESPONSE — a habit developed by doing the same behavior over and over again.

CUE-CONTROLLED RELAXATION — a relaxation response technique in which a student can relax himself by repeating certain cue words to himself. A good example of this is that upon hearing certain old songs (cue words) your feelings (emotions) often change.

DISCUSSION OF RULES — part of the modified two-column note- taking system. Students write down their lecture notes and important rules used to solve the problems presented in class.

DISTRIBUTIVE LEARNING — a learning system in which you spread your homework on a particular subject over several days instead of trying to do it all at one time. For example: Study for about an hour and take a five to ten minute break before continuing to study.

EFFECTIVE LISTENING — a behavior in which you sit in the least distractive area of the classroom and become actively involved in the lecture.

ENTRY LEVEL SKILLS — math knowledge a student possess when first beginning a particular math course.

EXTERNAL STUDENT — a student who believes that he/she is not in control of his/her own life and that he/she can not obtain his/her desired goals, like making a good grade in math. External students blame their teachers, parents — anyone and anything, except themselves, for their failures.

FEAR OF FAILURE — a personal defense mechanism by which a student puts off doing his/ her homework or he/she may have an excuse when he/she does poorly in or fails the course. Thus the student's real ability is never measured.

FEAR OF SUCCESS — a personal defense mechanism by which a student does not put forth all his/her effort to obtain good grades. Many students believe that by becoming too successful they will lose friends or may be expected to make good grades all the time.

GLOSSARY OF TERMS — a section in the back of a notebook developed by the student which contains a list of key words or concepts and their meanings.

INTERNAL STUDENT — a student who believes that he/she is in control of his/her own life and can obtain his/her desired goals — like making a good grade in math.

LEARNED HELPLESSNESS — a lack of motivation due to repeated tries to reach a goal (like passing math) but failing to obtain that goal. An attitude of "Why try?" develops because of numerous previous failures.

LOCUS OF CONTROL — the belief that one is in control of his/her own life, or that other people or events are controlling his/her life.

LONG-TERM MEMORY — the last part of the memory chain which retains unlimited information for long periods of time. It is considered to be a person's total knowledge.

MASS LEARNING — bunching-up all your learning periods at once. For example, trying to complete all your math homework for the last two weeks in one night. This techniques is an ineffective way of learning math.

MATHEMATICS ACHIEVEMENT CHARACTERISTICS — characteristics that students possess which affect their grades. These include previous math knowledge, level of test anxiety, study habits, study attitudes, motivation, and test-taking skills.

MEMORY — the process of getting information through your senses and storing the information in your mind. Recalling information for later use completes the process.

MEMORY DEVICE — a memory technique in which you develop easy-to-remember words, phrases, and rhymes, and relate them to difficult-to-remember concepts.

MENTAL PICTURE — a memory technique in which you visualize the information you wish to learn by closing your eyes and forming an image of the material in your mind's eye.

NOTE CARDS — 3" X 5" index cards; students write important concepts on the front of the card and an explanation of the concepts on the back of the card.

NOTE-TAKING CUES — signals given by teachers to their classes which indicate that the material they are presenting is important enough that the students may be tested on it. Notes should be taken on this material.

OVERLEARN -- continue to learn an already unerstood subject.

PERFECTIONIST — one who expects to be perfect at everything. This includes making an "A" in math when it may be, for him, impossible.

PERSONAL CHARACTERISTICS — characteristics students possess that effect their course grades, excluding entry skills. Some of these characteristics are anxiety, study habits, study attitudes, self-concept, motivation and test-taking skills.

PROCRASTINATION — a personal characteristic in which one puts off doing certain tasks, like homework, in order to protect one's self-esteem.

QUALITY OF INSTRUCTION — the effectiveness of math instructors when presenting material to students in the classroom. This effectiveness depends on the course textbook, class atmosphere, teaching style, extra teaching aids (videos, audio tapes), and other assistance.

RELAXATION RESPONSE — a learned technique which decreases emotional anxiety and/ or disruptive thought patterns. This allows you to think more clearly.

RE-WORKING NOTES — the process of reviewing class notes to re-write illegible words, fill in the gaps, and add key words or ideas.

SENSORY REGISTER — the first part of the memory chain that receives the information through your senses (seeing, hearing, feeling, and touching).

SEQUENTIAL LEARNING — a learning pattern in which one idea builds on the next idea. The ability to learn new math material is based on your previous math knowledge. Not knowing underlying math ideas causes gaps in learning. This often results in lower future test scores and even failure.

SHORT-TERM MEMORY — the second part of the memory chain which allows you to remember facts for immediate use. These facts are soon forgotten.

SKIMMING — the first step in reading a textbook. It involves reviewing a chapter to get a general understanding of the material.

STUDY BUDDY — a student who is usually taking the same math course as yourself; someone you can call on for help when you have difficulty doing your math homework.

TEST ANALYSIS — a process of reviewing previous tests for misread directions, careless concept, application, test- taking and study errors. Reviewing tests helps prevent their future occurrence.

TEST ANXIETY — a learned emotional response or thought pattern response. This response disrupts or delays a student's ability to recall information needed to solve the problems.

TIME MANAGEMENT — a process of gaining control over time in order to help you obtain your desired goals. Using a study schedule is an example of gaining control over time.

TOOLS OF YOUR TRADE — any materials you require to begin studying.

WEEKLY STUDY GOALS — the amount of time scheduled for studying each of your subjects over the period of a week.

REFERENCES

Reference A

MATH POST-TEST STUDY SKILLS EVALUATION

(USE YOUR OWN PAPER)

Read each of the items below. Check the appropriate column to indicate how often you comply with the statement. Seldom means 0% to 33%. Often means 34% to 66%. Almost always means 67% to 100%. Indicate what you *actually do* instead of what you *should do*. *Be honest*.

	Rarely	Often	Almost Always
1. I do not study math every school day.	☐	☐	☐
2. When taking a math course, I do **not** select a study buddy.	☐	☐	☐
3. Because I am relaxed, I remember important concepts during a math test.	☐	☐	☐
4. I study math less than 4 to 6 hours a week.	☐	☐	☐
5. I plan study time for math each week.	☐	☐	☐
6. When I take math notes, I do **not** copy all the steps to the problems.	☐	☐	☐
7. I use an abbreviation system when taking notes.	☐	☐	☐

	Rarely	Often	Almost Always
8. When I become confused in math class, I continue taking notes.	☐	☐	☐
9. I do **not** ask questions in math class.	☐	☐	☐
10. I do not quit reading the math textbook when I get stuck.	☐	☐	☐
11. I review class notes or read the textbook assignment before doing my homework.	☐	☐	☐
12. I do **not** fall behind in completing math homework assignments.	☐	☐	☐
13. After reading the math textbook I do **not** mentally review what I have learned.	☐	☐	☐
14. Many distractions bother me when I study.	☐	☐	☐
15. I do most of my studying the night before the test.	☐	☐	☐
16. I develop memory techniques to remember math concepts.	☐	☐	☐
17. I do **not** go to my math teacher or tutor when I have difficulty understanding a math topic.	☐	☐	☐
18. When taking a math test, I start with the easy problems in their numbered order.	☐	☐	☐

	Rarely	**Often**	**Almost Always**
19. When I have time, I check over my test answers.	☐	☐	☐
20. When my math test is returned, I do **not** analyze the test errors.	☐	☐	☐

MATH POST-TEST SCORING FOR STUDYING SKILLS

(USE YOUR OWN PAPER)

Put the correct amount of points for each item in Section A and Section B to obtain your score. The order of the items are different for Sections A and B.

SECTION A   POINT VALUE FOR EACH QUESTION

Items	**Rarely**	**Often**	**Almost Always**
	(5 points)	(3 points)	(1 point)
1.	_____	_____	_____
2.	_____	_____	_____
4.	_____	_____	_____
6.	_____	_____	_____
9.	_____	_____	_____
11.	_____	_____	_____
13.	_____	_____	_____
14.	_____	_____	_____
15.	_____	_____	_____
17.	_____	_____	_____
20.	_____	_____	_____
TOTAL	_____ +	_____ +	_____ = _____

SECTION B   POINT VALUE FOR EACH QUESTION

Items	Rarely	Often	Almost Always
	(1 points)	(3 points)	(5 point)
3.	_____	_____	_____
5.	_____	_____	_____
7.	_____	_____	_____
8.	_____	_____	_____
10.	_____	_____	_____
12.	_____	_____	_____
16.	_____	_____	_____
18.	_____	_____	_____
19.	_____	_____	_____
TOTAL	_____ +	_____ +	_____ = _____

_____ + _____ = _____

SECTION A   SECTION B   GRAND TOTAL

A score of 70 or below means that you have poor math study skills and need to read this book again to obtain its valuable information.

A score between 70 and 90 means that you have good math study skills, but you can improve by reviewing certain sections of this book.

A score above 90 means that you have excellent math study skills.

Reference B

TEN STEPS TO FOLLOW
WHEN DOING YOUR HOMEWORK

1. Before starting your homework, *read the textbook material* that relates to your homework. Pay special attention to the examples worked out for you in the book.

2. *Read and study your notes* paying special attention to any examples copied from the lesson.

3. *Do your homework neatly.* Remember, the neater you are, the easier it is for you and your teacher to follow the steps of a homework problem.

4. *Write down each step when solving a homework problem.* Writing down each step helps you to understand the problem.

5. *Try to understand the reasons* for doing each step of a homework problem. Do not just memorize how to do the problem.

6. If you are unable to do a homework problem, *follow these steps:*
   a. Review the textbook material that relates to that problem.
   b. Review the part of your notes that relates to that problem.
   c. Look in the textbook for any similar problems drawings, diagrams, etc. that relates to that problem.
   d. Call your study buddy.
   e. If another textbook is available, look for similar problems worked out.
   f. If you still can not solve the problem, skip it, but be sure to ask you teacher the next day how to solve it.

7. *Always finish your homework on a positive note* by completing the last homework problem. If you get stuck on the last problem go back and re-do a previous problem correctly.

8. After finishing your homework, *remind yourself of the purpose of the assignments*. Write down or recall the most important ideas covered in your homework assignment.

9. *Make up note cards* that contain problems that were especially hard or difficult to remember.

10. *Do your math homework every day*. It is important not to miss doing your homework. If you get behind you will not understand new material and will fail the course.

Reference C

TEN STEPS TO IMPROVING YOUR STUDY SKILLS

Improving your study skills can be a great educational benefit. By following these ten steps your grades can improve. Educators have proven that effective studying is the best way a student can improve grades. However, most students have not been taught how to study while attending elementary school, middle school or high school.

Students now have the opportunity to learn the difference between good and poor study skills. Educational research has shown the most effective skills required for good grades. These include note-taking, reading, memorizing, and reviewing. The following ten steps have been proven by research, and, when used correctly, will improve study skills.

1. *Do not study for more than one hour* at a time without taking a break. If, in fact, you are doing straight memorizing, do not spend more than twenty-five to thirty-five minutes. Difficult material should be learned in short study periods and reviewed more often. After studying for forty- five minutes to an hour you ability to retain material decreases. If you have been studying for two or three hours without taking a break, you probably will not retain the information.

Educators say you learn best in short study sessions. Spreading your studying time over several days is more effective than studying four hours in a row on the same subject. This is especially true when studying math. More time is required to understand ideas through practice between lessons. Spreading out your study periods over several days will increase your retention of that material.

2. *Find a good place to study.* When you first start studying, try to study the same subject in the same place at the same time. Select a quiet place at school and in your home to study.

After a while you will discover when you get to that time and place you will be already thinking about that subject. Training your brain to think math at certain times will decrease warm-up time. You will also save time and energy once required to get yourself ready for learning math. You will remember more math. After studying, reward yourself by doing something you want to do (watch television, go to a party). Experts know that positive reinforcement of a behavior (studying) will increase that behavior.

When beginning a study session, start with your hardest subject first and work towards the easiest subject. Your most difficult subject will take more concentration and effort. This requires a fresher and more alert mind. Less effort is required to learn easier material later on as your mind becomes tired.

3. *Do not study when you are tired.* Educators know that students have different times during the day that should not be used for studying. Do not study during that time. Discover the times you study best: morning, afternoon, or evening. Then schedule most of your study time for that part of the day or night.

4. *Separate the studying of subjects that are alike.* Your brain has a right and left side. Studying similar subjects one after the other will tire out the same side of the brain. This will decrease your study efficiency. Study math for an hour followed by English or history, not accounting or computers.

5. *Study for your classes at the best time.* You will forget most of the material learned in class right after leaving the room. *To best retain the material from the lesson, rework class notes or start doing the homework as soon as possible after class.* Prepare questions for the next lesson. Waiting two or three days to learn the same material will cause confusion and more study time.

6. *Use the best note-taking system* for you. For each subject, use an 8 1/2" by 11" spiral notebook with pockets to store handouts and old tests. Make sure your notebook has enough paper for the entire semester.

When your instructor lectures from the textbook, use the three-column system. *(Figure 18)*. Make a column two inches down the left-hand side of the note page for writing key words. The middle column should be made three inches wide and used for lecture notes. The right side

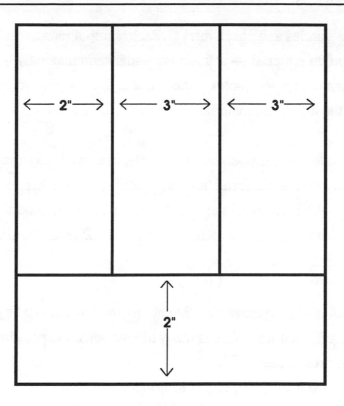

Figure 18
Three-column System

should also be three inches wide and be used for textbook notes. Put a two- inch space across the bottom of the page for a summary of lecture and textbook notes.

Leave several blank pages in the back of the notebook. These pages can be used for textbook words or concepts you did not understand while reading the chapter. Number and write a brief explanation of each concept or key work. Use the same procedure for each chapter. Review these notes as often as possible.

7. *Read and study the text at the same time*. How many times have you finished a reading assignment and could not remember what you just read? Researchers have found that it is more efficient to read and study at the same time. This procedure will take a little longer, but you will remember more of the material.

8. *Make up a symbol system for textbook and notes*. When reading your textbook, make up a symbol system to mark important materials for further study. The symbols can be boxes,

stars, question marks, circles and check marks. Each symbol represents a different message, such as: Very important material — star, do not understand material — question mark, and repeated material from textbook or notes - check mark. Developing your own symbol system will help you learn the important material.

9. *Do not use underlined textbooks*. If possible, use textbooks that are not underlined. Underlined textbooks represent information that another person thinks is important, not what you think is important. When textbooks are handed out and yours is underlined, ask your teacher if it is possible to have another one. If there are extra textbooks for the class, your teacher will probably give you another one.

10. *Use your full ability to memorize*. Do not memorize material by reading it over and over; this is the least efficient way. Use as many of your senses as possible when memorizing material. When memorizing ideas:

* Say the words out loud so you can hear them
* Record important ideas on cassette tape and play them back while you are relaxing
* Visualize the important ideas by closing your eyes and imagining those ideas in your mind
* Write down major ideas several times and say them to yourself
* Use association learning to tie in learning new material with information you already know. Relate personal facts such as your birthday with facts to be learned.
* Use acronyms such as ROY G BIV, which is the key to remembering the colors of the rainbow (red, orange, yellow, green, blue, indigo, violet).
* Use memory devices, which are phrases to help remember the order of different ideas. For example, the phrase, "Please Excuse My Dear Aunt Sally" represents the order of operations to complete a math problem (parentheses, exponents, multiplication, division, addition, subtraction).

All of the above steps must be followed to increase the chances of you improving your grades. Just using one or two of the above steps will not be enough to improve grades. Use all the steps and watch your grades improve.

Reference D

SUGGESTIONS TO TEACHERS FOR IMPROVING STUDENT MATH STUDY SKILLS

1. Show a film on test anxiety to students.

2. Help students learn to relax before tests are given.

3. Teach students how to take good notes in math class.

4. Emphasize that students should spend more time on math homework.

5. Encourage students to complete their most difficult homework assignments first. Usually, this means math homework.

6. Encourage students to read ahead in the math textbook in order to prepare questions for the teacher and make an informal outline.

7. Develop a dictionary of math vocabulary words.

8. Encourage students to keep a list of math vocabulary words in their notebooks.

9. Encourage students to develop study schedules and set up group study times.

10. Encourage students to construct practice tests and time themselves while taking them (prior to taking genuine tests).

11. Aid in developing the students' self-esteem so they will think about succeeding in the class rather than fearing failure.

12. Suggest that students do all the example problems in the text for practice.

13. Encourage students to write down questions for the teacher while doing homework.

14. Develop a list of professional tutors and share with your students when appropriate.

15. Make students aware of the time allotted them while taking a math test so that they may plan their work.

16. Discuss the importance of class attendance with your students.

17. Advise students to schedule their classes to leave room for study time.

18. Realize that students come to math class with different levels of math ability and that many students need extra help.

19. Encourage your students to come in, before or after school, for extra help.

20. Encourage students to verbalize (silently) problems the teacher writes on the board. They could then solve the problems or silently verbalize the methods of solution.

21. Encourage students to talk to you regarding their progress in your class.

22. Suggest that students make note cards to remind them of how to solve various math problems.

23. Advise students to get help early in the semester, should they need assistance, before they get too lost in the course.

24. Suggest that students recite back the materials they have read in the math textbook for understanding.

25. Suggest that students take notes while they are doing problems.

26. Tell students to copy all the information that is put on the board.

27. Recommend the book, How to Solve Word Problems: A Solved Problem Approach by Mildred Johnson or other appropriate books for use by students having difficulty with word problems.

28. Advise students to prepare for math tests through practice rather than memorizing.

29. Encourage students to do math homework every day.

30. Emphatically discourage missing math classes.

31. Remind students of their responsibility for materials covered in classes they have missed.

32. Encourage students to find a "study buddy" and encourage group studying.

33. Inform students about supplemental materials that may be of help such as other books, computer software, etc.

34. Encourage students to ask questions in class.

Reference E

EIGHT WAYS TO IMPROVE YOUR MEMORY

1. *Space your study periods* — Spacing study periods is better than learning material all at once. Long study periods make it more difficulty to remember what you have learned.

Time and spacing varies: three 1-hour periods result in better recall of material than one 3-hour session.

In the evening, you should study in short, spaced periods. You should then go to bed and get up the next morning and review what you learned the night before.

2. *Active recitation* — As you read and learn information stop often and repeat to yourself what you learned. Put into your own words what you have just learned. This will help you recall (remembering on your own) rather than just recognizing the information stored. If it helps you, write the facts down in outline form at the same time that you are reciting out loud the information.

Sometimes it helps to study with someone else. They can ask you questions about the information that you have just read or studied. Repeat out loud to them the important facts learned.

3. *Overlearn the material* — Continue to practice beyond the point of just remembering. Even though you are able to recall it once, continue to practice over and over again. This will increase the amount of material that you will be able to remember later.

4. *Recall* — bring back to mind something learned.
   Recognition — identification of something learned.
   Relearning — learning material that was learned before.
   Relearning is reviewing material learned earlier in the school

year in order to refresh your memory. This is better than cramming all at one time. The more you review during the school year, the less time you will have to spend going over old material for the test or exam.

5. *Use physical memory devices* — This means having other devices to remind you what to do or what to remember. These memory devices can be notes, calendar, lists, and people. Intelligent people use these memory devices to aid in the recall of information.

For example, to remember to do something when you get home, write a note to yourself and put it in your pocket. When you empty out your pockets the note will remind you to do what you wanted to do.

Another physical memory device is the "to do" list. This is a list of items to be done during the day. Check off the items as you finish them and add more items to the list as needed.

6. *Use mental memory devices* — This techniques may be one in which one or more words are made up of the first letter of each word of the information to be remembered. (Example: ROY G BIV represents the colors of the rainbow - red, orange, yellow, green, blue, indigo, and violet) or one in which easy-to-remember words, phrases, and rhymes relate to hard-to-remember ideas. (Example: In Please Excuse My Dear Aunt Sally, the first letter of each word represents the first letter of each order of operations - Parentheses, Exponents, Multiply, Divide, Add, Subtract.)

7. *Use association* — This means connecting what you want to remember with something you already know. For example, you want to remember the distributive property of multiplication over addition. Remember that distribution is associated with giving out a product. Then remember that multiplication is going to distribute its product over addition.

8. *Mental imagery* — This is used to form mental pictures of items or events you are trying to remember. To help recall an item or event, picture the place in which you learned it, imagine the surroundings, your feelings and even the place you sat. Also, to remember items or events, close your eyes and mentally picture the information in your mind's eye. Use mental imagery to remember and recall items or events.

Reference F

TAKING AN OBJECTIVE TEST

Multiple Choice - True-False - Matching

1. Before you start answering questions, preview the entire test. Survey the test to discover how many questions there are and of what type. Set a time limit so that you will have at least five minutes at the end to recheck your test.

2. Read the directions carefully, making sure you understand exactly what is expected.

3. Find out if you are penalized for guessing. If not, always guess and do not leave any unanswered questions.

4. Read each question carefully, underlining key words.

5. Anticipate the answer and then look for it. Read all the alternatives before answering.

6. Do not read into questions what is not there.

7. When your anticipated answer is not one of the options discard it and concentrate on the others.

8. When two or more options look correct, compare them with each other. Study them to find what makes them different.

9. Pass over difficult questions on your first reading and then come back to them after

completing those of which you were sure.

10. Use information from other questions.

11. In all questions, especially the true-false type, look for specific words that help determine your answer. Words such as rarely, usually, sometimes, and seldom allow for exceptions; never, always, no, and all indicate no exceptions.

12. Mark statements true only if they are true without exception. If any part of the statement is false, the whole statement is marked false.

Reference G

ANSWERING AN ESSAY TEST

Short or Long Answer - Fill-in-the Blank - Sentence Completion

1. Make a brief survey of the entire test. Read every question and the directions. Plan to answer the easiest question first, saving the hardest for last.

2. Set a time schedule and from time to time check your progress to maintain proper speed. With six questions to answer in sixty minutes you should allow a maximum of ten minutes per question. If ten minutes pass and you have not finished the question, continue to the next one and go back to it later. Do not sacrifice any question for another.

3. Read the question carefully. Underline key words: list, compare, define, etc. As you read, write down the points that occur to you next to the question.

4. Organize a short outline of the main ideas you want to present. Place a check mark alongside each major idea, then number them in order of presentation in your answer. Do not spend too much time on the outline.

5. In writing, always directly answer the question with the first sentence.
 Example: Explain Edison's theory of electricity.
 Answer: Edison's theory of electricity is based
on...
 The remainder is devoted to support by giving dates, examples, stating relationships, causes, effects and research.

6. Use material that reflects the teachers personal or professional feelings. Also, stick to the material covered in the reading or lesson and answer the question within the given frame of reference.

7. If you do not understand what the teacher is looking for, write down what you thought the question asked and then answer it.

8. If time does not permit a complete answer, use an outline form.

9. Write something for every question. When you "go blank" start writing all the ideas you remember from your studying. One of them is bound to be close!

10. In sentence completion questions, remember never to leave a space blank. When in doubt — GUESS. Make use of grammar and logic to help decide the correct answer.

11. If you have some time remaining, read over your answers. Usually you can add some additional ideas which may come to mind. You can at least correct misspelled words or insert words to complete an idea.

12. Sometimes, before you even read the questions, you might write some facts and formulas you have memorized on the back of the test.

Reference H

STUDYING FOR EXAMS

What to know before you start to study:

1. What type of test is it?

    a. Objective — multiple choice, true-false, matching, or a combination.

    b. Essay — short or long answer, or sentence completion.

    c. Problem solving.

    d. Combination of the above.

2. What material is to be covered?

3. How many questions (approximately)?

4. What is the time limit?

If the information above is not given by the teacher when he/she announces the test, ASK. This information is important to the way you study. Also, ask the teacher for old exams for your review.

STUDYING:

1. Be sure you have read all the material to be covered and have all the lesson notes before you begin your serious studying.

2. Plan what you will study and when.

3. Each review session should be limited to one hour. Take short breaks of five - ten minutes between hour sessions.

4. Try to predict exam questions. If it will be essay, try writing out the answers to your predicted question.

5. Study in a group, only if everyone has read the material. You do not gain as much when you must "tutor" someone else or if the other students are not prepared.

6. Prepare summary sheets from which to study to eliminate re-reading the textbook.

7. Review for objective tests by concentrating on detail and memorizing facts such as names, dates, formulas, and definitions (know a little bit about a lot).

8. Review for essay tests by concentrating on ideas, principles, theories, and relationships (knowing a lot about a little).

9. For problem solving tests, work examples of each type of problem. Work them from memory until you get stuck. Then study your example problems and begin working them again from memory from the beginning. Do this until you can work the entire problem without referring to your notes.

10. The day of the test, do not learn any new material. This can interfere with what you have already learned.

11. Try not to discuss the test with other students while you are waiting to begin. If you have studied, you do not need to be flustered by others making confusing remarks.

12. Try to consciously make yourself relax before the test begins.

13. After the test is over, do not waste time or energy worrying about how well you did. Start concentrating on your next exam.

14. Keep in good physical condition by maintaining a balanced diet and getting enough sleep.

Reference I

TEN STEPS FOR SOLVING STORY PROBLEMS*

1. **Read the problem enough times** -- enough times means the number of times it takes you to understand the problem.

2. **Decide what is given and what is being asked** -- all problems give necessary information and ask a question.

3. **Cross out unnecessary information** -- some problems contain extraneous (unnecessary) information.

4. **Begin to make a transition from words to symbols** -- start to write something on paper - draw pictures, diagrams.

5. **Use of a table might be helpful** -- some problems (distance/rate/time/mixture) require tables.

6. **Write a math statement (equation)** -- translate words into math symbols.

7. **Solve the math statement (equation)** -- use algebraic rules and concepts - do it carefully.

8. **Apply the answer from the equation to the story problem** -- for example: X=2 might mean that the width is 2 cm. or John is 2 years old.

9. **Check the answer in the story problem** -- answers checked in incorrect math statements may be wrong.

10. **Be sure the answer makes sense** -- for example: check an answer like 250 mph for the speed of a car - it is wrong.

Available in posters

FIGURES

BIBLIOGRAPHY

Bloom, B. (1976). Human Characteristics and School Learning. New York: McGraw Hill Book Company.

Fox, Lynn H. (1977). Women and mathematics: Research perspective for change. Washington, D.C.: National Institute of Education.

Ieffingwell, B.J. (1980). Reduction of test anxiety in students enrolled in mathematics courses: Practical solutions for counselors. Atlanta, Georgia: A presentation at the Annual Convention of the American Personnel and Guidance Association. ERIC Document Re production Service No. ED 195-001

Richardson, F.C., and Suinn, R.M. (1973). A comparison of traditional systematic desensitization, accelerated mass desensitization, and mathematics anxiety. Behavior Therapy, 4, 212 - 218.

Tobias, S. (1978b). Who's afraid of math and why? Atlantic Monthly, September, 63 - 65.

Wolpe, J. (1958). Psychotherapy by reciprocal inhibition. Stanford: Stanford University Press.

AUTHOR BIOGRAPHICAL DATA

Dr. Paul D. Nolting

Over the past 15 years Learning Specialist Dr. Paul D. Nolting has helped thousands of students and professionals increase their math test scores and obtain better grades — easily and quickly.

He is the author of two innovative books, Winning at Math and The Effects of Counseling and Study Skills Training on Mathematics Academic Achievement, and two cassette tapes How to Ace Tests and How to Reduce Test Anxiety.

Dr. Nolting holds a B.S. degree in Psychology, an M.S. degree in Counseling and Human Systems from Florida State University and a Ph.D. degree in Counselor Education from the University of South Florida. He is also licensed as a Counselor and a National Certified Vocational Evaluator. He is an instructor at Manatee Community College and the University of South Florida, president of the Ability Discovery Center, Bradenton, Florida, and a member of the Board of Directors of the Florida Developmental Education Association.

Dr. Nolting has also consulted with colleges, helping them improve mathematics academic achievement for their students.

A key speaker at numerous regional and national educational conferences and conventions, Dr. Nolting has been widely acclaimed for his ability to communicate with students on the subject of improving grades.

William A. Savage

William A. Savage has served education for over thirty years, having spent most of that time as a middle and high school mathematics teacher. His experience includes chairing a high school mathematics department, grades 7 through 12, chairing a high school mathematics department, grades 9 through 12, and serving ten years as a high school principal. Presently he is an assistant professor of mathematics at Manatee Community College.

Mr. Savage received his undergraduate degree at the State University of New York at Albany, N.Y., where he majored in mathematics and minored in physics. He earned his Masters degree in Mathematics Education from Union College, Schenectady, N.Y.

Throughout his career Mr. Savage has held many positions of leadership in professional organizations and currently is a member of the National Council Teachers of Mathematics, Florida Council Teachers of Mathematics, Sarasota Council Teachers of Mathematics, National Developmental Education Association, and Florida Two Year College Mathematics Association.

Mr. Savage has served as a consultant to numerous middle schools and high schools and has presented at state educational conferences. He enjoys an excellent reputation as a caring and dedicated teacher.

OTHER PUBLICATIONS FROM
ACADEMIC SUCCESS PRESS

BOOKS

WINNING AT MATH: Your Guide to Learning
Mathematics Through Successful Study Skills 12.95

THE EFFECTS OF COUNSELING & STUDY SKILLS TRAINING
ON MATHEMATICS ACADEMIC ACHIEVEMENT 29.95

HOW TO DEVELOP YOUR OWN MATH STUDY SKILLS
COURSE/WORKSHOP 8.95

CASSETTE TAPES

HOW TO REDUCE TEST ANXIETY 9.95

HOW TO ACE TESTS 9.95

WINNING AT MATH: Your Guide to Learning
Mathematics Through Successful Study Skills 9.95

STRATEGY CARDS

STRATEGY CARDS FOR HIGHER GRADES (3"X5") 4.95

STRATEGY CARDS FOR HIGHER GRADES (81/2"X11") 9.95

POSTERS

TEN STEPS FOR SOLVING STORY PROBLEMS 6.95

TRANSLATING ENGLISH TERMS INTO ALGEBRAIC SYMBOLS 6.95

TEN STEPS TO BETTER TEST TAKING 6.95

SIX TYPES OF TEST TAKING ERRORS 6.95

TEN STEPS TO DOING YOUR MATH/SCIENCE HOMEWORK 6.95

COMPUTER SOFTWARE

WINNING AT MATH: Computer Evaluation Software 49.95

SUCCESSFUL MATH STUDY SKILLS: Computer Evaluation Software 49.95

SPECIAL OFFERS

MATH STUDY SKILLS SUCCESS KIT 74.95

TEACHER'S MANUAL FOR WINNING AT MATH 8.95

TEACHER'S MANUAL FOR SUCCESSFUL MATH STUDY SKILLS 8.95